TIME FILTER

Brian M Thiesen

Best of Luck
Stick With It
You Are Your Future

Brian Thiesen

iUniverse, Inc.
New York Bloomington

Time Filter

This is a work of fiction. All of the characters, names, incidents, organizations, and dialogue in this novel are either the products of the author's imagination or are used fictitiously.

iUniverse books may be ordered through booksellers or by contacting:

iUniverse
1663 Liberty Drive
Bloomington, IN 47403
www.iuniverse.com
1-800-Authors (1-800-288-4677)

ISBN: 978-0-595-52889-9 (pbk)
ISBN: 978-0-595-62940-4 (ebk)

Printed in the United States of America

Ego, Reality, Eternity

Ego Must Exist Initially To Realize, Recognize Why It Must Die.
It Can Hold Your Reality In One Hand And
Hide Truth With The Other
It Must Desire More To Kill Itself Than To Stay Alive,
To Reveal The Secret It Knows But Hides From You.
It Is Something That Desires So Much To
Stay Alive But Is Willing To Accept Death If You Choose.
It Is The Centre Of Human Duality, But Not Duality As A Whole.
Before It Can Achieve Emptiness It Must Accept /Understand It.
The Ego Is God, The Master Architect
Of All Human Creation And Destruction.
But Without It There Is No Need For Either
Nor A Need For Humans As We/ It Knows It
Ego Is Impossible To Stop With A Closed Mind
Mostly Itself Keeps That Mind Closed With A Constant,
Fear Driven Need For Reassurance.
It Has Infinite Growth Potential,
Sadly Though, The More It Grows The Less It Knows What It Grows For.
It Is Reality, Its Own Reality, The Reality It Wants To See, Be, Is.
Its Reality Is The Complex And At The Same Time
Vulnerable Framework That Uses The Past
To Influence All Decisions.
These Decisions Are Made To Ensure
A Peaceful Satisfied And More Importantly
Secure And Somehow Deathless Eternal Future.
All The While Knowing It Is At The Mercy Of The Future.
It Is Fearless Of All Else Except This One Fact.
Because It Is The One Thing That It Cannot Control,
No Matter How Much Security It Surrounds Itself In.
This One Thing Creates Its Fear Mechanism
Which Keeps It Alive/Growing
A Growing Desire To Kill Fear But
With More Desires Comes More Fear,
Cyclical Until, Death.
All The While It Claims It Is Different When It Is The Same As
All The Other Egos Scared, Confused, Powerless, Ultimately Useless.
Trying To Surround Itself With The Power
To Protect Itself From Its Last Enemy, Itself!
It Makes Time What It Is,

Rather Than The Synchronized Artwork That It Truly Is.
Not Past, Present, Future But Merely Nothing, Emptiness
It Is All Three In One And When All Three Are Together,
Their Creation Is Nothing,
The Loss Of Everything That We/It Knows Exists
But From That Loss Comes The Truest Discovery Of All
When The Hiding Hand Disappears And The Light Is Revealed.
A Selfless, Timeless, Endless And Seamless World Of Emptiness.
Free Of Fear And Desire.
Truly What Is To Be Gained Is The Discovery Of A Soul
A Real Identity, A True Form Of Being In Its Purest And Highest State,
Broken From The Shell Of Ego,
Break Your Shell, Embrace Freedom, Witness Light, Discover Your Soul,
Become Eternity.

Conspirator Against, As I Conspire

All This That Conspires, At The Same Time Creates
At The End Of The Plan, Am I The Product Of Fate?
Am I Right To Feel I Have Little Control?
I Mean I Decide For Me But Not The World As A Whole
All That's A Factor Time, At Least Everything That's Happened Before
Walks In Me Soundless, But Not Ignored
Time Mostly I Obey, But Mostly For One Reason
I Think Time Controls What I End Up Being
Really It Mostly Prevents Me From Seeing
That No Matter What I Will Die
It's I That Controls This, Nothing Outside
Not The Gold In My Heart That Blackens My Blood,
Covers My Spirit In Hardening Mud
Not Everyone Else' Decisions Before, Future Or Now
Not The Control I Don't Have, But Finding Out How
To Make Time And Destiny My Own And Put Their Life In My Hands
Soon Fate And It's Conspirators Will Obey My Commands
This Self-Mutiny Must End If I'm To Play Deaths' Role
My Eyes, Hands And Senses Won't Get Me Out Of This Hole
My Mind And My Heart Must Connect With My Soul
Then I'll Be Walking With Time
Except Now In Complete Control

Emptiness, I

I Explore, Yet I Do Not Discover
I Ignore What Inside Is Covered
I Seek More From What Has Replaced My Mother
I Find No Beauty In This
Yet My Sword Is Merciless
In This I'm Not Alone But
I'll Always Feel Loneliness
Just Beyond My Fingertips
Is The Everlasting Kiss
That In This Life I Must Not Miss
Yet In My Heart I Resist
So My Feeble Mind Persists
Rendering The Depths Of My Soul Meaningless
Walk The Path Of Nothingness
When All I Need Is Emptiness

Constant, Constant

Realities' Constant Reflection In Front And Behind The Eyes
Simultaneously The Compounded Memories Of Each
Influences Our Every Move
However Seamless Seeming
It Is Far More Complex Than Required
A Loss Of Reality Is The Simplest Way, But Not Simple
A Greater Challenge Than Most Would Ever Know
Although Far Less Appealing;
Much More Satisfying
Truly Less Complexities Can At Least Satisfy The Minds'
Necessity To Make Room For More Distraction!

The Slave, The Master, The In Between, The Flawless Stone, A Beauty Yet To Be Seen

I Ask, And His Response Is;
"Not If, But How, Not When But Now"
"How Will I Find What Does Not Exist?"
"The Search Makes It Exist"
"So It Is Concrete?"
"Yes. But Even Concrete Can Be Molded And Carved"
"So I Am Not Stone?"
"Yes You Are. But Only In Every Moment Appreciated/Experienced"
"So I To Am Carved?"
"Yes Eventually Until There Is Nothing"
"Death?" I Ask
He Replies "Yes. Your Body And Mind"
"What Else Is There?"
"You"
"Is This What I Carve, Chisel A Stone To Nothing, Death?"
"Are You Afraid?"
I Reply.
He Says "Your Hammer Has Never Existed.
For It Could Not Even Be Used If It Did."
There Is An Invisible Layer That Must Be Broken"
"Continue"
"Like A Shadow It Is Only Seen With Some Light But
Only Exists With Darkness. It Hides There. And
From This Vantage Point Calculates Your Every Move
Without Your Approval. Only When The Light Is All Encompassing,
Will The Shadow Fade."
I Pause. "Go On"
"Only Then Can The Sculptor See What It Is He Sculpts And
At The End Of His Creation,
His Goal Is To Know He Makes Nothing At All, And
What Actually Exists Is Only What Cannot Be Seen With Eyes"
Now The Only Logical Reply Is The Sound Of Hammer, Chisel And Stone

Defeat

Much In This Life I Have Done
Much In This Race So Far I Have Won
The Establishment, System And Authority I Can Claim
To These I Have Learned And Mastered Their Game
Dodging Obstacles, Facing Adversity, And Using Pain
Rising From These Leaves Me Nothing But Gain
My Strength Built Up For Any Task
My Mind To Sharp To Be Fooled By Mask
A Master Of My Life, Therefore Life Itself?
Hardship And Strife Trophies On My Shelf
Illusions Abound But Not So, As These I Can See
When I Do I Thank Myself For Being Me
I Calculate Risks And Play The Odds
In Defiance Of Paths Set Out By Gods
My Channel Is Right And That's The Way I Live
If I Am On The Side Of Right
What More Of Myself Should I Give?
Through This All A Sense Of Humility
Failing For A Second Brings Sense Of Futility
Yet In All This Winning I Still Seek Answers
I Sing My Song But Am A Songless Dancer
I Have Walked Thousands Of Miles, In Dozens Of Shoes
Through All My Winning I End Up With More To Lose
In No Way Have I Announced Defeat
Still In No Way Is My Life Complete
Cause Through It All I Have Still One Enemy
It Is Myself, Failing To Be The Self I Want To Be
What I Want Is Far From Losing And Winning
It Lies In The Peace I Lost From The Beginning
It's Up To Me To Reclaim My Fate
This Reclamation Must Not Wait
For In This Waiting My Soul Will Enter It's Gate
An Abandonment Of An Achievable Peaceful State

Destiny Is The Past?

Destiny Is The Past
Destiny Is Nowhere?
Everyone Knowingly Or Unknowingly
Decides At Each Moment Their Direction
Toward Goals Lofty Or Meek
Collectively And Successively Until Death
Which Is A Common We All Share, The Other Being Time.
If Time Is Shared By All Then I Am A Part Of Time
If Time Is A Part Of Life, Then I Am Time, I Am Life.
From This Time And Life
I've Come To Realize That At An Unknown Time In Life,
My Life And Time And Therefore Life And Time Itself
Will No Longer Exist
If My Past And Life Itselfs' Past Make Up The Future And
In That Future Is My Death
Then All I Do In The Present Is Live In A Constant Moment
With Life And Death
Slowly Until The End
When Life's Time Ends And Death's Life Takes Over
Using Numbers To Label And Show How Close I'm Getting
When In Reality I Can Get No Closer Than the Present
Only Labeling Not How Long I've Lived But
How Much Present I've Experienced
In The End Experiences Lead Up To My Death
Like All Other Life And
If What I've Experienced Is My Death
Then I've Decided To Be Dead My Whole Life

In Between Two Dreams, Two Loves

One Far Behind But Close Enough To See
One Too Far Ahead At Least That's What It Seems
Where Is A Man When He Lies Between?
Some Would Say Nowhere, I Must Agree
For There Lay My Body But My Soul Never Sleeps
Not For Lack Of Self Love Or Regret And Self Hate
But In Agony Of What's Been And For What Now I Must Wait
Patiently Now, But Patient Long Enough
Patient How? For One Day Is Too Much
Put Those Days Together And Patience Wears Thin
Pull Them Together And I Still Won't Be Where I've Been
Do Nothing And I'll Remain In Between
Doing Something Got Me In The Shape I'm In
This Shape Is What Will Make Me Do It Again

End The Pain

Find The Pleasure To End This Pain
A Found Pleasure Is Pain Born Again
Only This Time Stronger Than The Child Before
The Infant Mind Remains At War
No Amount Can Cure This Ill
The Pills We Swallow Hopeless Until
Our Skin Is Wrinkled And Our Bones Are Weak
These Scars We Bear, Unscarred Are The Meek,
Is What We Read And Say We Follow
As We Look Our Hearts Grow Hollow
Whatever We Find Is Surely To Swallow
Our Mind And Body Like Our Spirit Already
Not The Quickest But Slow And Steady
We All Know We've Questioned Why
Only We Use These Eyes
Clouded And Consumed As Time Goes By
This Question Strongest The Moment We Die

Too See Life,

If I Could See My Death,
If I Could See My Afterlife,
If I Could See My Before Lives,
If I Could See My Life.
So To See Afterlife, Utopia, Say.
Would I Live My Life Differently Today?
Could I Still March With Evil? Fearlessly?
So To See Afterlife, Hell, Say.
Would I Change My Life Today?
Would I Attach Myself To Good?
Do I Know This Path? Even Where It Starts?
Does Anyone? Self Discovered I Guess
Would Before Life Reveal Lives Unchanged?
If For Common Good I Guess I'll Not Complain
My True Needs And Societies Are Not The Same
Is The Time For Change Now Or Even Needed?
For Constant Change Can Still Be History Repeated
Could I See My Life? I Guess I Can Now
'Cause Now I'm Looking At All The Ways How
To Change My Life Or Stay The Same
To Approach Each Day With Undying Aim
To Find A Life Inside This Game
Not Any Life, The Life Of This Man
To Change My Life I Will Live Each Day The Best Way I Can!

The Awakened Soul

Much is said about heart and soul and their
Connection and correlation.
However, not much is spoken about the
Heart of the soul and its correlation
With living a fulfilled life or living a full life.
Our soul feels, lives our experiences.
Our experiences are our souls' life.
Truly it is as much a part of us as air, water and
All other things that allow us to live but
Anyone can breathe, anyone can drink and anyone knows
That they must do this in order to continue to live.
However, the distinction between being alive and
Living is not known by all.
Whether it is chosen by those not to obtain _it_,
Impossible for them to obtain _it_,
Or their fear of obtaining _it_ and losing _it_ are the questions
It is _it_ that awakens the soul.
It is _it_ that is the only Real motivation for any action.
Also it is _it_ that is the heart of the soul.
As well if you (your soul) is not in your heart
Then you will never find _it_ and
Even when _it_ is there you will never see _it_.
However, when (if you are capable of it)
You do see _it_, you do taste _it_, you do feel _it_,
It is then you will thirst for _it_,
It is then you will require _it_ like the air you breathe.
It is then you will know you have _IT_.
It is then you will know you are alive.
It is then you will know your soul has been awakened.
It is then you will know you are in love.

Couragermination

Our Need For Pleasure Causes Both
Internal Pain (Self) And External Pain (Others)
Can I Convince Myself That Taking Away Pleasure
Will Take Away The Pain Of Others?
If Others Continue To Indulge,
Should I Embrace The Burden They Create Within?
This My Seed Of Courage, Nurtured By
The Unfound Nutrients I Possessed All Along But
Left Unturned By The Shovel I Never Carried;
Until The Day Convinced
I May Lose Conventional Pleasure But I Will Also Lose The
Universal Pain
Was This Not My Goal Anyway?
Have I Become This Blind? Better Yet Senseless?
Now The Harvester Of A Fruitless Crop
As I Continue To Starve By Feeding
On The Rocks That Hide Truth Beneath
Shutting Off My Senses In The Satisfaction
I Will Live Another Day
In What My Brain Calls Life
My Heart Calls Futility And
My Soul Calls Death
My Soul Forever Crying Enough Tears To Feed Infinite Crops
Until It Cries No More
Either By Death Or The Harvest Of Courage

Destruction

I Am Destructions Everlasting Feast.
I Am The Machines Most Important Part
I Am Loss' Truest Advocate And Pains' Trusted Ally
Lost Within A Lost Race
Lossed Before My First Pace
Everything I've Wanted Has Lead Me This To Find
Now This Is All I'll Leave Behind
A Past Fed Future 'Til The End Of My Shallow Book
Like A Dream The Pages Dissolve The More I Look
So To The Future I Look Instead But
They Still Dissolve
Like The Endless Dream That I'm Already Dead,
Because The Dream I'm Thinking Of Is My Life Instead

A Second Life

Seconds Can Define A Mans Character
A Second Can Be A Lifetime
A Second Can Linger Over A Lifetime
A Second Can Overshadow A Lifetime
A Lifetime In The Shadows But Not In The Dark
What Defines Or Sets Apart
Merely Seconds And What's True To Your Heart
Seconds Passed Over Discarded, Erased
Seconds Memorable, Not Time But Place
If A Second Ago Was The Case
Every Second From Now Is Your Backwards Race
Funny How Forward Could Make You Go Back
Keep Looking Backwards Its All That You Get
In Case You Haven't Figured It Yet
With All This Looking Its Hard To See
Every Second That Is Presently
Waiting To Be Seen With Happiness Or Sorrow
Heads Down We Walk And Ponder Tomorrow
Every Second Accepting The Lasts' Wrath
If You Don't Look Up You'll Miss The Whole Path
On A Journey Of Seconds Times Ticking Fast
A Lifetime Of Seconds
One Second Closer To Its Last

Dream It Be Possible

What Is The Succession Of The Dream?
The Ability To Dream, Or The Ability To Achieve?
For Many Can Dream Big, Even The Biggest
What Is The Root Of Our Passion? And Where?
Can This Root Permeate To
Our Inabilities And Make Them Capabilities?
Or Does It Grow Only First Knowing Capability?
The Variables Align In Perfect Order
Why A Fixation On A Goal Of Good Or Evil Intention?
Why To Stagnate On Nothing At All?
Daily Compounding, The Symphony Of Our Life Composed
Only We Can Hear Its' Perfect Entrancing Melody
Do We See Others As Perfect?
Aspiration Born To Be But Impossible To Become
Unless Becoming Is Of One Self's Perfection
Is That Not The Dream, The Passion, The End Of The Root?
Capable Of Good And Evil
The Succession To Perfection
And Then What?

Express

To Somehow Express Outwardly The Make-Up Of Our Mind
Is This It For Us?
Am I Really Confused Enough To Need To Prove,
To Affirm To Myself Who I Am?
As If There Were A Mirror In Front Of Me At All Times?
Do I Accept/Embrace Myself?
Am I In Love With Me?
Is This The Basis Of My Actions?
Is This My Actual Actions?
Or Now If This Is Not True; What Creates The Need To Project?
For Upon This Action The Proof
That True Self-Love Is Not Present
Show, Display, Impress, Care, Is This Not Natural?
No! A Display Shows Potential To Self-Love But
The Presence Of Confusion
Lies In The Need For Others To Confirm
A Reason For Me To Love Myself But
Who Can Look At Me And Say I'm Worth My Love?
Who Can Say I Love Myself Enough?
Further Upon My Death Who Can Confirm I Loved Myself?
Surely Not Those Who Look To Me For The Same Answers
 Not Even Knowing They Ask The Questions
Amongst All This Can It Really Be That Hard To Love Oneself?
Truly? Of Course!
For Amongst Those We've Known Who Has Achieved This?
Who Have We Witnessed?
You Wish You Knew One, You Wish You Were One
This The Guide To Your Blind Life
That Someone Is Watching But Just Can't See!
Stop Wishing And Be

Young Dream

Youth How Do I Hold/Keep Thee?
I Ask Permanence In Your Embrace Of Me
One Day Though, I'll Wake To A Memory
Realizing There Is Another Picture To See
An Aftermath Of My Reality
Momentary Appreciation Can Only Be
Realized/ Experienced In The Future After Youths Passing
What Will I Become? What Have I Become?
If I'm Right Now, I'll Be Right Later
If I'm Wrong Now, I Can't Expect Later
Judging Now I Expect Something Greater
Than The Pieces Combined To Complete This Puzzle
In The Hope That This Will Solve
The Most Perfect Dream I Call My Life.

Pursuit

The Pursuit Of Everything Is The Path To Nowhere
In The Race To Be Someone We End Up Like Everyone
How Much Longer To Immortality?
As Death Approaches I Look Past His Eyes
My Life In Focus But It Shows Me Lies
My Soul Left Alone Slowly Dies
If Only I Could Hold This Everything, Even Just Once
For I Have Earned It,
Don't You Think?
Then Again So Have You
I Don't Know What More I Can Do
Always A Bit Faster Yet Still I Pursue
The Chase, My Life
I Wade In Strife
Treading Water To Keep My Head Above
Ignoring The Benefits Of Self-Love
True Life At My Fingertips
If Only My Actions Mimicked My Lips

DRUGS

Get As Far Away From Myself To Find Myself
However, As Soon As I Run I Can't See Myself
I Worry Not, As I Will Meet Myself Like So Many Times Before
But Strange I Can Only See Myself When I Get Back
This Time I'll Surely Like What I See When I'm There
The Prophecy Now Clearer
But The Promise Closer To Reality
Where Is Reality?
If The Prophecy Is Clearer How The Path Lightless?
This Now Scarier Than The Catalyst Of The Journey
This Was To Be The End Of Fear, Comfort Everlasting!
My Final Detachment From The Cause
Now I Know A Path
Now I Know What Draws Me Closer
Now I Know Where I Run
Yet I Do Not Know Where To Run Or Why
The Answer Lies In The Same Head That Asks The Question
Up Until This Insight, Reality Is Trampled By Footsteps

Evil Become

Living Evil, Dying Evil
Pretending, Pleading Innocence
Or Worse Begging For Mercy Or Worse Still Placing Blame
Consistently Graduating From Level To Level
How Many Are Enough?
What Is Enough For Each Level?
As Much/Many As It Takes
Until I Can Wrap My Hands Around It, Savor It
Somehow Enough That It Can Become Part Of Me
Although Not Possible, Deeming It Worthy Of Just Celebration
In Celebrating Now Evil Is Condoned
Your Morals Allow Evil, You Allow Evil, You Are Evil
We All Can Deny This But The Truth Is
We Want To Deny That We Should Look
At Ourselves Seriously To See
The Fact We Do This Means There Still Is Hope To End It
To Continually Recognize And Go On
Means Your Life And Evil Forever Intertwined

Within, Without

A Look, For Once, Finally, But Not Final
The Look Is A Choice, But Only One
The Moment Is The Choice The Only One
You Are The Choice, The Vital One
Ignore The Voice And Speech Is None
Become The Action, Action As Life
Become An Action, Live In Strife
For In An Action There Is Much
Not All Action Needs Movement, Especially This
For This Is The Action Until Now That Was Missed
A Look Within To See What You Were Without
For As Much As You Wanted You Lost To Doubt
Now It Seems You've Figured Out
Without Within, You Are Within Without

Kings War, Peasants Journey

Upon Possessing The Earth The King Looked To The Sky.
Upon Assessing Worth, His Soldiers Marched High
As They Marched The King Asked Why
For All Before Manifested Have Become A Lie
For If It Were Truth Then Long Ago Marching Ceased
This Feeling Of Gain Matched By Decrease,
In The Worth Inside Him And The Time He Has Remaining
He Owns It All But Has Not Been Gaining
Through All This War It Is For Peace He Has Tried
With Each Step He Walks Further Outside
Of The Peace Only Found With The War Won Inside.

Present But Undefined

What Is This Without
Label, Number, Reason, Quantification, Description?
What Is This That Defies Logical Explanation,
Justification, Common Perceptual Properties?
In Trying To Name We Also Create Gravest Of Injustices,
It Asks Simply For Acceptance For It Already Calls You And I Home
But Would Also Like To Be Recognized As A Guest
Crying From The Bottom Floor, The Deepest Parts Of Us.
We Know Its Depths Already,
They Can Still Become Deeper, As Deep As We Desire
We Have Mutual Control Of Each Other But Not Total Control.
We Both Share Time, But Know Time Separately
Us As Our Time, It As All Time
It Cannot Reveal Immediately How It Controls The Time
Yet Gives Us The Ability To Do It
Although It Knows Before Us How We Will Use It Even In Change
It Knows Especially In Recognition / Rebirth Of This Underlying,
Undeniable Self-Hidden Knowledge What Will Be
If Only Uncovered, Then It Can Be Held To Light,
Us Being Light When We Are Combined
Through Belief As A Mutual Craving
For Each Other Creates What Before Was
Poorly Defined As Something Besides,
That Now Is The Bond, God State.
It Is Not Secret For It Has Been Before Man
With Man And Will Be After Man
It Is Just That; Uncovered, For The Biggest Thing Imaginable
May In No Way Be A Secret,
Merely A Cognitive Perception Based Illusion
That Must Be Perceived By Other Means Than The Five Senses
To The Men That Discover.
The Infinite Is Possible, Including Becoming Truth Through Virtue
The Common Man May Use The Word Soul
The Men Of Truth Just Become The Definition

Ice Water

Wait For The Clean, The Clean To Fall
Wait For The Water To Clean It All
Fresh My Eyes, Fresh My Soul
Fresh My Mind, Make Me Whole
You Are Welcomed, But Still Wait For Acceptance
My Arms Are Open And So Is My Mind
Wash Me Clean, Clean My Will
Accept My Hand And Walk With Me
Instead Of Stepping Back And Walking Away
Now I Cannot Trust Although You Are Clean
Because You Don't Trust Me
I Step Back Into Accepting What Must Be
I See The Water And In It I Even Bathe
Cleansing My Skin Cleaning My Head
However It Is For Something Else I Long For Instead
Not My Skin And Flesh, Not My Head Nor Even My Mind
Merely All The Stuff I Want Left Behind
Bring The Water, Fall Through My Soul
Take My Life Into Your Control
Alas Your Approach But You Hesitate
Is There Still Something In Me For Which You Wait?
You Are A Mirror And Yet I Can See Through

Making It Harder For Me To Know What To Do
Now Finally You Grasp My Hand And Lean To My Ear
Only To Tell Me What I Don't Want To Hear
That I Am Like You, See Through And Clean
To Look In The Mirror And See What You Mean
Yet When I Look All I See Is Black
All I Want Is To Look Back
To Look Forward Is What You Ask
Looking Back A Feeble Task?
For Doing This Is What Makes Me Weak?
In Doing This I'll Never Seek
To Be What I Can Instead Of Was
As Of Now To Know That I Am What I Am Not Because The Water Is Shy
Or That I Can't Go In And Only Ask Why
I Can't Change Or You Won't Help
Because The Change You Offer Will Not Do
Until I Change Me And Then Look At You
And With A Sadness But Still A Sharp Smile
I'll Stand Proud With Myself For A While
At A Lost Vision Of Your Sea
For I Won't See It Because It Is Now Me

Always Something,

Always Something To Do,
Always Something To Look Forward To.
How Much Now Does That Leave You?
How Much Of This Will We Go Through?
Carry On Forever Realizing
When We Look Ahead We Lose Some Things
Sometimes Those Things Are The Most Important Of All
The Distance Growing Still Can't Fade Its Call
Because It Rises Up Inside Your Mind
Will The Path You Choose Follow All These Signs?
Or Will You Leave It To The Stars To Realign?
To Give You Back That Feeling So Deep
The Same Feeling That Now Won't Let You Sleep
Because You Lost The Only Thing Everyone Should Keep
Maybe The Sleep Is Better Than Awake
Your Living Dream Is What You Now Face
Where To Find Someone To Take My Place
The Place Inside That's Dedicated To
Everything That Reminds Me Of You
And All The Thoughts That This Creates
Ponder My Path Of Crucial Mistakes
Because I Thought True Love Never Breaks
I Guess It Does But I'm Still Attached
Because I Know Our Love Was Unmatched
We Move On Yes, But To Where?
Now That We're Here We Wish We Were There
In A Time That's Not So Far Apart
A Time That Gave Purpose To Me And My Heart
You Are My Heart And My Heart's In Your Hand
Awaiting The Day It And Its Soul Meet Again

Infinite Blindness

From The Depths Of Emotions Thoughts Seem To Rise
A Rarity When It Comes To Optimism
Do We Not See The Greatness That Is Before Us?
For The Actions That Bring Forth Have Long Since Passed
The Same Can Be Said In Sadness Though
Is It The Fear Of Permanence?
What Are The Thoughts To Make It Disappear?
Or Is Disappearance Understanding?
When Are We To Understand Happiness?
Or Secretly Do We Know It Impossible
At Least On This Path
Knowing Sadness To Be More Constant, Do We Seek Solace
In Prevention Through Knowledge
Thereby Which Opening More Doors
To The Happiness Never Found
For From Previous Behaviour Have We Not Learned
We Will Never Find This Door
In Constant Search Have We Outlined The Map
To The Depths Of Hope?
Or Confirmed The Value We Place On Infinite Blindness?
For It Must Be Asked, Where Has This Map Led Us Before?
The Answer Is Nowhere And Exactly Where We Are
Open Your Eyes

Time Machine Me

A Constant Focal Point And Fulcrum
Always Moving Controlled Or Forced
Thought Woven, Action Crafted
Pushing Through Seconds Changing Them, Molding Them
Time, Where Is Your Importance?
Ultimately Your Contribution Is To Life As Is My Life To You
You Know How Long My Clock Will Tick
I Wonder If You Know This About Yourself?
It Must See The Action Unfold Just Like Us
Because In That Is Why We Live
For The Emotions/ Reactions Caused And In Those Seconds
The Feelings Risen; To Know We Still Feel
We Can Feel A Reason To Keep Pushing, A Justification
Imagine If Your Feelings Stopped
Evil, Love, Fear, Desire Whatever
That's It! You're Nothing
Rendering Actions Toward Utopian Mortality Non-Existent
Now Usefulness Fades As The Idea Does Not Manifest
Its Elusiveness Only Makes The Craving Grow
The Apex Of Utopia More Shadowing Over Time
The Focus Shifts To Estimate Worth;
Meanwhile On The Outside Time And Reality Have Not Changed
Just You And How You Feel/React To This Problem
Although The Past And Future Are The Product,
The Underlying Equation Remains Unsolved Purposely.
For This Unanswered Question Is The Birth Of All Feelings
The Sole Excuse We Continue With Time
For In The End We Could Choose To Discontinue Time And
Feeling, In One Second No Less
Neither Of Us Want That For We And It Are Both Trying To
Get The Most Out Of Our Lives; This Focus Shared,
Dually Piercing; Creating An Opening
To These Feelings We Crave To Somehow Induce Rebirth

Dead Search

Still Searching
For What I'm Not Sure
Maybe For Belonging
Maybe For Certainty
Maybe For Direction
For Purpose, Meaning, Reason
Is The Fact That I'm Searching My Purpose?
Or Is Not Finding It Yet My Flaw
Will I Ever Find My Purpose?
If I Cease To Search Will I Still Be Living?
I Can Still Be Living But May Not Be Alive
Then To Stay Alive Is My Purpose
This Search Keeps Me Alive

Belief, Heart

Why Do We Believe?
Because There Is Nothing Better To Believe
We Need An Explanation, A Truth, A Reason.
We Can Neither Stand Miracles
Nor Looking At Ourselves, But Others Did.
Guidance Is Essential But It Can Only Be That,
Thoughts Are Ours To Use They Must Be Used Carefully
For They Create Our Reality What We Believe,
Morals And Therefore Actions
Our Beliefs Tell Us Which Way To Go Mostly Ignoring Our Heart
On A Quest For Oneness,
Fulfillment That Only Lies In That Heart.
Ignored To Long And It Becomes Weak,
Ignored Forever It Never Existed.
Refuse Ignorance And Rejoice In Your Heart
The Only Belief Worth Fighting For.

Attic Of An Addict

So Deep, Deep In My Heart, Deep In My Mind
It's Become, It's Becoming, Now I'm Becoming
The Deeper I Get, My Shallowness Equal.
From Non-Existent, To Experiment, To Requirement
What Gives It Precedence?
How Does It Stay In Front?
How Do I Remain Behind?
Because I Want To.
For I Am Become And
Will Always Be
But Its Not Inside, It Must Enter Me
The Less It Does The Closer I'll Get,
I Have Become But I'm Not Finished Yet!

After Before

Afterlife… Wait After Death… Wait 'til After Death
Use One Life To Prepare For The Rest
Life Is Not Judged At The End But During
Knowledge, Thought, Action Not Quite The Same
Intention And What Unfolds, (Reality) The Game
Why So Scared, To Repent Before Death Is Enough?
How About Nothing To Repent?
Besides To Whom Do We Offer This Weaklings Prayer?
If So Weak How Could A Higher Power With Godly Stature
Find Worth In The Time Taken To Hear Our Pathetic Words?
For If Answers Were To Be Given Why Not Sooner?
Why At All? Especially Now?
Your Last Words And Days
Not Even A Fraction Of What's To Be Judged
Yet Forgiveness Begged For The Mistakes, Mistake Of Your Life
Appeal To No Response No Answer But Hear The Echo In Your Soul
The Voice That Speaks Loudest,
Your Past, Will Collect These Words Too
As It Always Has, And It Still Won't Change
It Still Can't Be Taken Back
You Had Your Time
Is Your Position Now The Symbol Of Its Waste?

Suffercate

Imagine Suffering
What Do You Think It Would Be Like?
Take Your Problems And Measure Them Up To Others
Well At Least You Are Better Off Than Them
Better Off? Really, How So?
What Do They Suffer From That You Do Not?
Time? Disease? Fear? Desire?
In That Way You Are Identical
Do You Breathe, Eat, Talk, Better?
Are You Really Better?
Or Like Time And Disease
Do You Not Also Share Confusion, Insecurity, Pain, Mortality?
You Know It But You Do Not Want To Contemplate It
For If You Do You Become Equal
More Money, More Distractions,
Distracting You From The Thought Of Death
Distracting You From Your Life,
Creating Fear And Uncertainty
Your True Common Understood Now; A Weak Mind
Your Closest Bond The Equaling Link
That No Possession Can Break And
Only Love Can Sever
The Choice Becomes Love Or Suffering
This Choice Becomes You

Taxed Path

Avoid Decision And Uncertainty
Despite What They Have To Offer
Stick With Routine And Comfort And
What They Take Away
Lead Me To The Dream I May Never See
Prepare Me For Tomorrow
I'll Do The Same
I'm Used To Getting Used To It Now
Only Memories Of Youth When Each New Day Was Just That
Instead Now Another Day Just Like The One Before It
This Is Tomorrow?
Somehow This Is Done/ Accepted By Most
Drain Yourself,
Slowly,
The Slower It Gets, The More You Lose
Until The Game Is Over

The Dance

Black River Banked White In Snow
Golden Sunshine Tempts Ocean Blue Glow
Clouds Heart Falling Magnifies Ill
Loves Heart Calling Makes Time Stand Still
Tears To Swell Eyes As Coffin Is Sealed
Tears Eclipse Smiles As Baby's Eyes First Revealed
Fruit Peeled Flawless Dies Purpose Served
Seed Drops Lawless But Ancestry Preserved
Bullet Strays To Pierce Mans Soul
Kindness Exchanged Genuine Fills Deepest Hole
Darkness Sought Out Through Devils Eyes
Light Pierces, Divine Truth Conquers Lies
Violin Stroked Awakens Despair
Words Choked In Beautiful Woman's Eye Glare
Mating Call Made Without Consummation
The Sorrow Dwarfed By The Smallest Constellation
These Inseparable Partners So Far Apart
Yet Would Not Survive Without, Like Bloodless Heart
This Dance I Witness Inside And Out, Who's Song Goes On
Which Played Before Me And Will Long After I'm Gone

Biography-Epilogue-Epitaph

Procreate- The Mass Production Of Destruction, Constantly
This Spells Impending Doom
As The Fight To Stay Alive Kills Us All
Acceptance Of Insignificance Rather Than
Thoughts Of Importance Is The Saviour
For I May Seem Important To Me
To This Race I Am Not.
As A Whole With Me The Numbers Increase
Not Necessarily The Strength
For This Only Increases By The Decrease
In My Destructive Capabilities And Needs
Whose Correlation Is My Exterior Consumption
It Is Symbolic Of My Lack Of Strength
And Will To Be Consumed By Love Instead
The Real Pillar Of Strength,
Killer Of Doom, Significants' Trophy,
My True Birth, The Gateway To Importance,
The Saviour Of This Race And
At The Same Time The End Of Mankind
As We Know It, But Not Our Extinction

Search

Search Soul, Find Hole
Fill Hole But With What,
Emptiness You Say?
Sounds Impossible; To Me Anyway
They Say Reality Is Perception
I Say Reality Is Reception
What We Want To Receive
What We Chose To Believe
Because Of Reception We Must Believe
Because Of Perception We Are Deceived
Oddly Because Of This Deception Our Mind Stays Relieved
Our Soul Sits And Waits
For Our Mind To Clue In
That To Believe In These Lies
Is Mortal Sin
Truth Of The Matter Is Reality Is Lies
To Connect With Your Soul You Can't Trust Your Eyes

The Poets Poem

A Talent For Some, A Solace For Others; Always Natural
Where Do They Come From?
We Don't Know
We Do Know They Can't Stay Inside
Not For Long Anyway
Sometimes They Beg To Leave
Sometimes They Wait Around A While For Refining
Alas, Polished, The Creation Imminent
A Storm To Furious To Pass By, Unleashed
The Result The Fading Of Loneliness
Procreation To Share, Be Shared
Step Into My Storm, Better Yet Become It
Stop Now, You Are Not In Control, I Am
My Rain, Your Seed, The Plant Is Now Up To You
Where Will You Go From Here?
I Know Where I'm Going
To Chase The Storm
I May Not See Another
The Cloud Is Somehow There, Natural
I Beg For Solace, I Call The Storm
My Talent Forever Influenced By The Storm On The Outside
My Words The Cloud That Never Dies

Innocence With Guilt

Proclaim Your Innocence, Denounce Your Guilt,
Claim No Control In A World Someone Else Built.
Locked Inside Your Mobile Cage
The Book Is Burning And You're The Next Page
You're Not The Subject, The Root Of The Blame
We're All Human But We're Not The Same
For You Are Different, It Is They Who Are Evil
Your Mind The Rock, A Temple To Admire
Living In The Shadows Of Your Desire
Just A Little Is All You Need
Just A Bit More Cannot Be Greed
You See The Future You Cannot Be Blind
Is Possession The Key To Your Perfect Mind?
The Sad Part Is The Lock's Always Changing
Wandering Around Looking For Keys
The Object Before Was The One That Was To Please
The Last Thing Needed To Fill The Hole Inside
Only To Find The Object Lied
Not To Worry The Next One Will Provide Bliss
You're Not The Only One That Will Go Through This
Turn Off The Light And End Another Day
Lay And Think Of Tomorrow Like You Did Yesterday
What Has Changed But These Thoughts Gaining Strength
What Has Grown But Your Eyes' Surrounding Wrinkles' Length
Now Those Eyes Are Closed And Welcome Dreams
A Vacation From The Struggles And Schemes
An Escape From It All Until The Alarm Clock Rings
Sit Up With Your Head In Your Hands Pondering
When Your Real Life Will Bring Relief
Each Hour Passing Fades Belief
That Waking Life Could Mirror Your Sleeps'
Harvesting Memories Worth Trying To Keep
Is A Tough Thing To Do When You Seek Perfection
With Eyes Alone It Avoids Detection
The Problem Is Its Dark Inside
Justified Actions And Souls Collide
Often It Is The Soul That Loses
Sadly It's What Your Action Chooses
Ignoring The Souls Purpose Altogether
Makes Another Day Become Forever

WAR

My Contribution To Continuous War,
Up To And Including Complete Extermination
How Could This Be?
Ask How Many Other Species Have Been Exterminated?
How Many Races, Ethnicities Have We Virtually Eliminated?
Yes You Are A Part Of We One Way Or Another
Blindly Condoning These Acts, Or Worse Looking Away
As Men Die For Your Pleasure, Maybe Profit!
We Fault Their Leaders But Fall Short Of Doing Anything Significant
After All My Voice Is Heard Every Four Years Or So
Complain, Blame And Then Sit Back And Change The Channel
Think Of How Intelligent You Are,
Where The World Would Be Without You
Better Yet If You Ruled It
Truth Is We'd Be Better Without.
For If Ruling Can Exist We Do Not Live In A World
Let Alone A Free One
We Live Inside A Hole In Society
Upon Command We Perform, Upon Demand We React
For Personal Benefit Of Course, With Reasoned Good Intention
This Good Intention Helps Shelter/Hide The Guilt.
Who Gets Hurt Along The Way? Other Humans Of Course
More Importantly, Yourself,
You're Just So Used To It That Sadly You Don't Feel It.
The Gift Of Life Slowly Fading Like The Directions On The Map
You Once Drew With Pride,
This Now Leads Two Steps Behind Your Coffin
At All Times,
A Continuous War Created Inside Becomes Your Outside World
Just Like All The Rest And If We Are All At War
The Only Result Can Be Extermination
There Is One Way Out And Its Not Death
Nor Is It The Life Your Living Either

Broken Or Alone

The Choice For My Heart
I Am Lured In By A Magical Start
Only To Realize I Was Misled
A Walking Story Millions Have Already Read
When I Turned The Last Page I Was Back At The Beginning
It Once Was A Game Always Worth Winning
Now I Look Back And Start To Think
I Read The Book Without A Blink
Sadly Now My Eyes Are Still Open
A Bottomless Heart Is Painfully Hoping
For A New Book To Appear But Where Will That Get Me?
To The Final Page Only To Let Me
Realize I'm Back Where I Started
To Walk Among The Broken Hearted
A Loveless Heart Will Never Bleed
Yet Why Do I Still Need To Read?
Knowing Fully The Consequences Of My Actions
For A Split Second Of Loves Satisfaction
I Guess Loves That Powerful To Blind And Confuse
My Heart Is The Only Thing I Have Left To Use
I May Win Now But In The End I Will Lose
Unless My Heart And Self Love Are One And The Same
Then There Will Be No Time For Blame
For There Will Be No Need For Time If There Is No Game

How's Life

How Are You Treating Your Life?
Life Is Not Treating You For It Did So Upon Your Birth
A Stage Must Be Found To Propel Constant Maturity Or Mire
In Diluted Fraud Calling Upon Others To
Blame And Others More To Cure
If We All Do This We Will Have Unturned All Stones
Yet Still Shutting Our Eyes Upon Doing So
The Answer Is Deeper, A Common Refusal To Look
Proves Our Egos Futility
Reliance, Its Birthright, Natural, Addictive
A Calculated Toll With Deadly Results, Mostly Premature
Amazingly Thrilled At Glimmers Of Hope So Much Are We
That Collectively A Disease Is Created
Wishing For A Cure, Stability, Security The Answer, God
Something External Please Help Me For I Am Only Human
What Could I Possibly Do But Remain Useless
In This State I Pray Not To Die
Although My Actions Fearfully Welcome Death
A Second Birth Must Be Created Within
Not So Much A Total Realization, But At Least Thought
That Something Greater Exists Besides A Stale Mindset Of Endless
Thought To Become Whole
With The Acquisition Of Exterior Pleasure
True Bliss Hides Itself Because It Wants To Be Looked For Properly
It Is Masked Yes, But Its Mask Can Be Removed
At This Moment It Will Speak And You Will Realize
All Words Before Were As Useless As You Were
Only Then Will You Know What You Were Looking For
Coincidentally And Simultaneously
All Searching Perishes Under The Discovery Of True Life

Jackmind

We Are Numb, We Are Blind
Watch The Fake Lives Unfold
While Missing The Only One That Is Real
Just To Tolerate What Next To Buy
With Every Thirty Seconds We Become More Fake
Than We Could Imagine
The Ones Imagining For Us Have Seen
This Reality Before, After All They Did Create It
Your Reality Is Fantasy, You Must Begin To Hate It
So If Your Going To Sit There And Stare A Mindless Stare
Look Inside Your Mind Instead And Take Back What's Not Theirs!

The *WAR*rior

A Warrior Lies Inside But His Heart Is Weighted By Demons
Although Almost Dead,
The Heart Struggles On Waiting For Something Important
To Unleash The Warrior While His Sword
Should Already Be Drawn;
He Sleeps In Contentment But Does Not Bathe
In The Happiness At His Swords' Tip
Because The Sleep Is The Extent Of The Warriors Needs
The Heart Must Bathe In The Blood
At The Tip Of His Relentlessly Refined Sword
To Awaken To The Death Of His Last Demon
Bringing Witness His Own Birth
The Opposite Is The Death Of A Warrior But Not A Warriors Death

Journeys End

Sure You're Getting Older, And Maybe You Feel Wiser
Who Knows? Maybe You Actually Are
Realistically Your Expansion And Mind Growth
Has Long Since Been Completed
Life/School, You've Learned Your Language, The Language Of Numbers
Through All These, Your Capabilities, Physically, Mentally, Overall
So Now You've Come Across Situations (By Choice)
From These Variables Presented; Calculated And Manipulated
Your Variables In Order To Produce The Most Favorable Outcome
Or At Least Avoid Negative Outcomes.
So Now You've Learned To Dissect Experience
Further Somewhat Control Them Through
This You've Gathered Memories, Also Noble
Does This Equate To Growth Though?
Have You Not Lately Questioned This?
Of Course You Have!
Where Is The New Growth, Expansion?
Moderation Of A Thought Process From Within A Question
To Seek Something Deeper Than Manipulation Against Fear
Surely This Is Not The Limit Of My Capabilities?
By Choice Maybe But Not By Misinformation.
Where Do I Grow Then?
What Growth Do I Seek?
When Will I Be Complete? I Hope Before Death
Will I Know If I'm Complete Then If I Reach This?
What Is The Definition? Personally And As A Whole?
Beyond Passion, Being, State.
Tell Me Who Will Be My Guide?
Who Will Light My Tunnel?
Letting Me Continue Down Lighted Path
For If Not Seen It Cannot Exist
My Growth Has Lead Me This To Believe
This Sadness Sought With All My Being
Soon The Manipulation Will Be Of Me
Or Is It Already? Of Course!
However, My Tunnel Awaits, Truly The Real Path Of The Wise
The Light To Wisdom The Eventual Growth
That We Are Capable Of No Beneficial Growth Unless Spiritually Achieved
This Can Still Be The Greatest Satisfaction Provided On What Was Once
A Hopeless Journey Ended Long Ago

Momentence

Moments In Time, Out Of Time
In Me, Out Of Me
With Me, Without Me
A Path To Clarity; Steps To Rejoice In
How Perfect Is Life?
It's Not You Say, You See…
No I Don't It Is You That Sees, Or Perhaps Not If One Disagrees
As Words Life/Perfection, Thought/Connection
Do Not Always Fit.
A Word We Know To Well Is The Simplest Explanation:
Choice
As Listed All Of Theses Have Opposites:
Fear, Disbelief, Disorganization, Despair,
Weakness, Unworthiness, Deprived
Fortunately No Man Need Face These Perils
In Facing Can Choose To Remain Controlled By,
Or Emerge Stronger From All
The Requirement; One Moment, One Thought,
One Belief, One Desire,
One Man.
One With All These Is Limitless, Boundless
In His Hands Dream Like Potential
Countless Are Those Who Reason Against
Time And Again Are Controlled
Self Blinded, Though Surrounded By Light
Helplessness For The Masses
A Pure Gift Toward Light Lead Perfection For A Select Few
One May Ask
"To Which Moment Shall I Look For This Light You Describe"
The Answer Is
The Moment At The End Of This Sentence

Nothing Satisfies

If Nothing Satisfies
Why Do I Want Everything... Anything?
Surround Myself In Security
Buying My Insides
Creating An Environment Outside That I Want Within Me
While All That Is Within Me
Is Working To Make This So
Security With Myself And My Surroundings
Surrounded By Comfort And People Who Bring Comfort
People I See Myself In Or Part Of Myself In
Maybe Its Our Sense That Together
We Can Create A Mutual Security Within Ourselves
Or Is It To Find That We Are Less Secure
Security Itself Is Defined By Our Insecurity
Correlated With Fear To Avoid What
We Can't Or Don't Want To See
Most Of The Time What We Don't Want To See,
Is Ourselves

Beauty In Men

There Is Beauty In Men But Not Mankind
Mostly This Beauty Lies In An Uninfected Mind
Possessed By The Young Soon To Be Tainted
By The Same Brush That Got Us Painted
The Colour Grey Stale And Old
This Colour Has Variance But Will Always Be Cold
However It's Not This Bleak Unless We Let It Be
No We're Not This Weak We Just Choose To Be
The Success Of Our Ego Overshadows That Of Our Spirit
It Cries From Deep Down, But We Just Don't Hear It
Sure We Listen But Find No Use In Changing Now
Strange That We Think When Instead Of How
If We Knew How We'd Probably Still Wait For When
But When, When Comes We'll Wish We Were How Way Back Then
The Regrets Pondered By A Youthless Mind
The Time Squandered By A Ruthless Kind
Ignorance And Arrogance Our Life's Glaring Trait
An Unloved Soul Can No Longer Wait
To Accept Desires' Undesirable Fate

Judge This

Who Are We? Who Are You? Who Am I?
The Last One To Be Judged
By The Most Important Judge; Me
Save Myself Until The End, When Is The End?
I Know, Never, So Why Should I Judge Me?
Surely Others Do Not; How Could They I'm Perfect?
From What I Can See Anyway
I've Done The Best I Can From What I've Been Given, Right?
Now Next Case, Next Person
Idiot, Stupid, Clueless, Loser
That's Them, That's Their Label.
They Had The Same Life As Me,
Why Can't They Be As Good As Me
Why Can't They Change Themselves, Their Life
Take Me For Example; Look At Me, See Me
Judge Me Surely You Will Find No Flaw,
No Error, For I Am The Judge
I Can Judge All People And Doing So Makes Me Better
Asking Me To Change Would Be Asking Me Not To Judge
If I Didn't Judge Who Would I Be?
Who Would You Be?
Flawless?
Maybe Not, But At Least Then I Could See

Motivate

Do You Ever Question What Motivates You? Is It Worth It?
Is It Worthy Of You? Is It The Most Valuable? To You?
Is Your Mind Clear ?
What Are You Looking At Then?
Does It Look Back And Laugh?
Or Are There Too Many Clouds Obstructing?
Do You Think Of The Outcome Of Your Actions?
The Pain They Might Cause? The Joy You Could Bring?
Both Inside And Out
Now Is It Worthy To You?
What Now Is The Outcome Of Your Thought?
What Now Is The Motivation?
What Now? Is The Question
What Is Your Action?

Long To Be Awakened

Only So Long To Wait
Even Waiting Is To Long
Long Enough To Be Forever
The Longer Waited, The Closer To Never
I Long Now, But Only To Wait
I Long To Blossom But It May Be To Late
Not Long To Live,
Not Long Replaced,
Not Long Before Longing
Becomes Reality's' Face

Can I Have Wants?

We Want What We Can't Have
We Don't Want What We Have
Even If What We Have
Is All We Could Ever Want
The Tragedy Of The Human Mind
No Parallel Can Be Drawn
No Explanation Granted Worth
Yet In This Paradigm We Live
Our Minds' Sight Fades With Each Shallow Goal Upon
Accomplishment We Wonder The Merit Of Our Action
Questioning Still Our Need
However The Lack Of Answers
Somehow Links The Chains Of Self Slavery
Freedom Measured As A Physical State
Mental Freedom Long Ago Broken; Agonizes
Knowing That This Too Is Our Fate
This Being The Majority Should In No Way
Extinguish The Shame Of Our Expendable Shallowness

Kingdom The Power,

Is A King More Fearful Of Death
Or More Desiring Of Life?
For Is This Shaping Time? Or Is Time Shaping It?
You Must Be Evil, Crave Possession
While All Perish Around You
Worry Of Crumbling Walls Instead Of Crying Souls
Including Your Own
Creating Suffering For Personal Gain
All Wealthful Gains Lost In The Process Of
Trying To Create Them
Surely It Seems Right,
If It Is So Right Why Must We Continue?
If It's So Right, Why Do We Question?
We'll Feel Better Not To Think About It
So Bring The Next Distraction
The Curtain Down On The Questions
While We Take Back To The So-Called
Comfort We've Enjoyed Until Now And
The New Ways We Can Secure It
Problem Is Once It's Been Secured
It's Not Worth Securing Anymore

See You There

Show Me Your Struggles, I'll Show You Mine
Show Me Your Failures, I'll Do The Same
Show Me Your Fear, Mine Is Equal
Show Me Your Pain, This Too I Possess
Show Me Your Path, Strange Here We Are
Your Desire Is Before Me, Mine Likewise You
Show Me Who You Are, For Both, This Will Be Tough
Show Me Your Inside, Can You? Can I?
Show Me A Dream
Be Your Reality, See My Reality
Live In My Dream
Not Quite What I Seem, Nor You
Seems We Both Have A Dream We Both Have A Heart But
Our Hearts And Our Dreams Are Too Far Apart
Scattered Footprints Until Now
Must Become The Steps Of Dreams
A Clouded Dream Before, Much Closer Now It Seems
Hope To Get There And See Your Face
Dreams Never Awake Unless Our Fears Are Displaced

SoulPathy

Where Am I?
How To Find Me?
Follow My Path Not Straight But Narrow
Winding With Crossroads And Forks In The Road
Choosing Directions As Only I Know
My Daily Life The Clues And Keys
To Guide Me To Eternity
Will I Answer Or Turn The Keys?
To Solve The Mysteries That Clear Eyes Can See
Or Shall I Walk The Shallow Road
That Like So Many Others Leaves Cold And Alone
Blinded, Misguided, Distracted And Drown,
Mentally Confused, Nowhere But Down.
What Is The Answer?
Which Way To Go?
Looking Down The Path I'll Never Know
That What Exists Deep Inside Is The Only Road
A Solo Man Walking Is Never Alone
Because That Man, Walks With His Soul

Stroke Of Chaos

A Simple Artist
A Careful Eye Monitoring Delicate Art
An Ever Changing Picture
Still Requiring Its Sole Frame
Colours Appearing And Fading As Quickly
The Most Colourful Lasting Longer
Yet Still Hazed By An Evergrowing Fog
Barely Balancing On The Past, Present, Future Tightrope
After A While Becomes Easy
The Program Initiated Has Now Grown
Into A Thought About But Mostly Automatic Reaction
Although Constantly Changing,
By How Much Is Now Questionable
The Journey To An Outside Force
Ends In Front Of A Mirror With The Leader Asking
Where Am I Now?
His Eyes Soaked In Fear Now Knowing It Was A Waste
These Journeys Compounded, Overlapping
However Adventurous, End In Misery
Questions Begged To An Outside Force
The Result, A Chaos Erupts Inside
Exposing It As Hollow
Rendering The Framework Useless And Its Artist Stale
Through The Constant Change Of Nothing At All.
True Art Possesses No Frame
Nor Does The Artist Himself Possess But
Is The Owner Of One Thing
A Masterpiece That Is Never Finished Still Seeking Its Final Stroke
In The Mean Time
Preparing For The Picture Only His Eyes Will See

The Man On T.V.

What Do We See?
What Do We Look At?
What Are We Looking At?
What Are We Looking For?
What Do We Genuinely Care About?
Do We Care About Ourselves?
Do We Care About Our Self?
Are We Even Thinking At All?
What Do We Think When The T.V. Is On?
What Are We Watching For?
When Has A T.V. Shown Love?
When Has It Laughed, Cried, Lived, Died?
Is It Really That Hard For Us?
Is It To Hard To Hear, See, Feel Truth?
To Feel Pain, Discomfort, Fear?
Is It Really Comforting Then To Have No Emotion At All?
What If It Were A Human?
Would You Love It So?
Would You Give So Much Time To Him?
Would You Care When You Throw It Away
In A Few Years Knowing You Can Buy
A New One To Serve The Same Purpose?
Would You Not Be A Slave Master?
Or By Giving Your Time, Life, Energy,
To Something With No Reward
Financially, Physically, Emotionally, Spiritually
Is It Not You Who Is Being Mastered?
Is It Not You Who Is The Slave?
A Slave Who Stares At His Master Daily But Never Sees Him
Merely A Reflection Of Him That When It's On Is Lost In Space
When It's Off The Master Revealed,
A Man Who Bares His Exact Face.

Greatness Is,

Greatness Is As Much A Level As It Is A Feeling
For Because Of This Feeling We Become Addicted To Greatness
We Push Ourselves Down A Path
Regardless Of What Lies In Our Way
Caring Less About What Lay In Our Wake
This Wake Can Only Be Seen In What We Were
The Bearing Of The Past On The Present And
This Marriage The Conception Of The Future
The Future Being The One Thing That Can Cure Our Addiction
Achieving A Certain Level Or Height
Once This Peak Is Reached Then The Summit Can Be Seen
Only That We Have Been To The Summit Before
Strangely Enough It Is The Peak We Now Stand On.

Conception

Constant Stimulation Lust Breeding With Itself.
Conception Being Our Identity Which Is Misperceived Uniqueness
Fueling An Unquenchable Desire. Our Need? The Fuel.
Then By This Definition Our Reward Is
A Fear Filled Undesired Death
Strange How We Could Desire Fear,
Yet It Seems If We Use Ego As Our Eye
We Convince Ourselves This Is Not So
By Recognition Of This Are We Not Compelled
To Destroy It's Desire? Which Is Fear
In This, It Is Then Known
There Is No We If There Is Ego
For If We Are To Be Love
There Is No Room For Fear

Memory

Got A Memory Of What I Was
But I Don't Know Who I Am
When I Did It Was 'Cause
Someone Made Me Give A Damn
For Our Love I Would Have Died
Now That Love Has Left Me Dead Inside
I'm Alive But I Cannot Live
Cause You Don't Want The Love I Give

Got A Memory Of Where We Were
But I Don't Know Where We Are
All The Memories Make It Worse
And They Won't Get Me Very Far
Another Love And Another Broken Heart
Everything I Knew From The Start
I'd Like To Think I'm Smarter Than Before
But I Know I'll Do It All At Least Once More

Got A Thought Of Who I Could Be
But Until Then I'll Search Inside Of Me
Still I Won't Change What You Don't Need
Stabbed In The Heart Yet I Do Not Bleed
What I'll Be Will Be My Best Of All
Despite The Past I'll Answer Loves Call
Although At Times It Feels Less Than A Lie
I'll Find The Truth Before I Die

Mind Frost

My Shadow Callused By Frost
The More I Look, The More I'm Lost
Paying A Price Of Endless Cost
These Words I Write The Only Passion That's Real
Although All My Actions Choose
Something I May Never Feel
Without These Actions I'd Have Nothing To Write And
Although Briefly,
My Hand Allows My Soul And My Mind To Reunite

Pen Light

As My Pen Is Stroked, Light Flickers On The Wall.
The Words I Write Flicker In Us All
The Flame It Precedes Awaits Ignition Call
Off Lit Path I'll Surely Stray But
Always Come Back To Stay
Others Opinions Will Not Mine Sway
In My Quest To Be The Light Today
My Soul Knows No Other Way,
But To Hold Dear And Be The Words I Say!

Our Life,

Our Life Is Made And Meant For One Reason,
That In The Time We Are Given,
We Find Out The Reason We Are Given So Much Time
Most Of The Time This Is A Passing And Unexcited
Pondering Of How Things Will Get Done
Instead Of A Passionate Thought Of
Why They Are Their To Be Done And What Are Their True Benefits
So Easily Are We Entranced Into The
Exploitation And Criticizing Of Others
Telling Our Self That In Comparison To Me
This Individual Is Lacking In Most Or A Certain Area
In Some Cases It Is Naturally True And Just For Us To Think,
Believe And Know This.
However, In Most Cases It Is The Most Feeble Of Ways For Our Minds
To Shield Ourselves From Our Own Shortcomings
Of Greater Significance, This Shield Allows Us To Become Complacent
Reasoning Ourselves Into Not Changing Improvable Deficiencies
Thus Creating A False Increase To Our Confidence
Developing The Illusion That We Are As Good As We Can, Will Be
Disabling Our Being Of Achieving Full Capability And
Enhancing Our Minds Ability To Collapse Before Fear
Letting Your Mind Kill Your Soul Before Time Kills Your Body
Enabling Us To Fall From Living To Existence Knowing
What We Desire And Knowing We Are
Better Than Those Individuals Around Us
Also Knowing The Reason We Are Surrounded By Those Individuals
Is We Chose/Choose The Same Path By Fear
Not To Become Different From Them
Or The Same As Someone Who Has Already Achieved What We Want
In The End We All Achieve The Goal Of Life,
The End Of Our Time, Our Death
We Must Become Masters Of Our Time, Our Death
For It Is Because Of Death Our Entire Life Is Molded
Through A Desire To Be Or A Fear Of *Becoming*
If We Knowingly Lived In This Fear
Then All We Really Desired Was To Die!

Hell Immortal

How Come Our Egos Got So Big?
We're Really Scared.
What Made/Makes Us So Scared?
Fear Is The Feeling
Why Do We Feel This?
Self Preservation, Short Term, Purely Physical
Touch, Hear, See
Preserve Yourself From The Past Trials And Tribulations
Dually Closing Your Mind And Opening Fear
Creating Motivation Against Pain,
However Pain And Its To Real Belief
Creates Its Power To Want To Be Avoided,
Its Real Power Is To Still Manage To Appear
After Much Effort, Mostly When Least Expected!

My Time

Passing Time, Pass It To Who?
Killing Time, Killing You?
Wasting Time, Can You Afford?
Finding Time, Once Ignored?
Making Time, Now What Will You Make?
Taking Time, Yours To Take?
Losing Time, Tell Me Where Does It Go?
Out Of Time, How Could You Know?
Time Of My Life, Going So Slow
Time To Live, Inside This Time
Time To Live, This Time Is Mine
Time To Live, This Time Its Time!

Life IS Yours

Life Is The Game That It Takes You Through
The Closer You Get To Your Coffin The More You Realize
What You Did Isn't Necessarily What You Should Do
The Only Natural Thing You'll Ever Know
When It Gets Here Its Time For You To Go
Although Until Then It's Been Ahead Of You
This Is The Place You Lead You To
The Bliss Sets In What A Joyous Moment
Don't Be Afraid Now; It's Life You Made Scary
Embrace The Partner Now That Before You Only Danced With
Pull It To Your Heart And Give It A Kiss
Thank It Now For Its Gentleness
However Unexpected Its' Timing Is Right
Maybe Not All Your Decisions Brighten Your Past
Somewhere You Decided Tomorrow Would Be Your Last
What A Gift All The Years Leading To This Moment
A Gift You Must Accept But Can Never Own It
Still It's Better Than Any Other
More Than A Product Of Father And Mother
The Proof Lies In Our Fate
We'll All Walk Through The Same Gate
Even If It's Not Heaven Our Souls Still Can't Wait
All This Time A Fear Of Being Alone When We Die
A Lifetime Spent Turning The Truth To A Lie
Before You I Lay With Closed Eyes
With You I Lived A Life That Never Dies
Until You Join Me One Day
Then We'll Both Be The Words That I Say

Lossency

You Know Not Loss
Merely A Dependency
On An Attachment That's No Longer Being Fulfilled
You Know Withdrawal
Sometimes Brought On Suddenly Or Over Time
If This Is Known Then Wouldn't Its Prevention Also Be Known?
It Appears Not.
As The Attachments That We Bear So Many Scars From, Increase
This Becomes Inevitable
As This Accomplishment Of Self-Fulfillment
Becomes More Lustworthy,
Although Through Attachment It Has Never Been Achieved

Pride Is Not Learned It Is Inflicted Naturally,
Reinforced In Solitude And Celebrated With Humility But
Never Confused With Self-Fulfillment For If Genuine
Its Own Denial Is Paramount

The Seed Of Destiny Is Possession
It Is Also The Seed Of Destruction
Except When The Truth Is The Desired Possession
Possession, False, Temporary
Ego's Feeble Attempt At Mortality
Soulmate Of Blindness, Gatekeeper Of Truth.
Possess Truth, Possess Self, Possess Love

Looking Around

Looking Around But I Can't See Love
I Now Look Inside And Then Above
It's All I Want I've Had A Taste
My Soul Left Hungry, The Next I Won't Waste
Give Me A Chance, Surely You'll See,
A Heart That Thirsts To Find Use For Me
More Important Get Back What Was Taken
To No Longer Stand Among The Forsaken
The Most Important Gift Only Two Can Give To Each Other
To Never Need Or Think Of Another?
That Feeling Inside That Overshadows The Rest
Without It Living Becomes Survival At Best
You Are The One That Makes Living Real
Others Could Try But Can't Make Me Feel
The Way You Do Without Even Trying
The Most Valuable Feeling, To Valuable For Buying
Is What We Made While We Were Together
Its So Deep Inside But It Can't Be Forever?
Now Anymore Time Would Be Better Than None
When Our Hearts Are Together, Our Souls Become One
One Day You'll Look Around And I Hope That You'll Be
Taken Back To The Only Place Worth Trying To See,
Hoping The Heart That Takes You Is The One Inside Me

Mind Valium

What Does A Mind Cost?
What Is Your Minds' Worth?
What Are The Moments You Give Worth To?
What Are The Moments You Bring You?
Are They All You Hoped For?
Or Could The Price Have Been A Little More?
Too Late Now You've Already Conceited
Those Years Of Your Life; Your Being Depleted
The Chemical Bond Has Already Been Formed
The "Living" You Has Already Been Mourned
Still Contemplating Your Value Or Price?
Stepped On A Mirror Turned Out To Be Ice
That Cracked Upon Your Life's Last Step
Unlocking The Secret All Those Who Died Had Kept
That To Place Value On The Mind Is The Worst Thing To Do
To Value Yourself Every Single Moment Must Be Worth You

Money,

Money killed its creator.
Its power his passion, Greed his drug, Misery their sum
Is it king?
You deny it but still bow.
How slowly it comes in,
How quickly it goes out
Leaving you wanting more
Making you get more
Fulfilling your life by letting you enjoy less of it?
Realize if you are working for it
Or if it is working you for it
Know that it can work for you
The less you think you need it
First understanding what it is you want
Letting what you want blind you from reality
It is the hole in your past,
Is it the whole of your future?
The invisible but present master
Its blindfold pulled tighter with time.

Miracle

Not A Man But A Miracle
Not A Man Of Miracles
A Miracle Of Man
The Miracle Me
I Am The Miracle You'll Never Be
However Remove Your Best Deeds
You Still Might Beat Me
Without Good Intention Do I Deserve Me?
Define The Word Or Does The Creator Do That?
Devine, Your Knowledge But Your Actions Half That.
Miracles Can Happen But What Do They Teach?
What Will We Learn?
Our Actions Will Display What Our Mind Wants To Say
To All The Rest Of The Miracles Around,
The Miracle Me Speaks Without Sound

One Day, Today

Every Day One Is Harder To Do,
Without A Day One How Can There Be Two?
Will This Be The Last? That's Up To You
Or You Can Go On Doing What You Want To Do
The Wasted Life Your Living Through
If There Was A God It Would Destroy You
Oddly Enough You Probably Would Too
Instead Do It Slow And Pretend You Don't See
They Have The Nerve To Criticize Me
They Don't Know My Life And The What I've Seen
When Your Face Is On Their Screen,
It's What You Are Not Should've Been
Some Lives Are Perfect, Some Lives Suck
One Things For Sure, There Is Always Luck
Fortune, Luck Will Never Come Around
To The Ones Whose Lives Are Bound
By Outside Substance And Inner Addiction
While Those Around Exercise Prediction
You, My Friend, Are Your Own Affliction
Sympathy Only Lasts So Long And Goes So Far
For The Common Man It's Very Hard
To Look At You And Feel What You Feel
A Shallow Life With No Appeal
At Least Have The Courage To Kill Yourself
Maybe Start Over As Someone Else
By Loving Yourself And Looking Inside
Because Before You Know It, Someone Else Will Die!

Destroy

Take, Take, Take More, More, More
What Happens To All Animals With Appetites?
How Come What We Want Is So Slowly Punished?
We Are So Used To Wanting;
Soother It's Beginning, Now Here
It Must Be Acceptable Then (It's Been So Long)
I Don't See Any Consequences, Nevermind Harmful
What Do I Take To Make Me Happy,
Encourage My Existence?
What Makes Me Go On?
I May Take Only A Little But It's Constant
Collectively Now, Yes! All Of Us Do It
Take A Little Piece, Go Ahead
What About Those Who Take Big Pieces?
Just Think How Much More They Want
More Big Pieces To Take
Aren't You Doing The Same?
Bigger, Just A Little More, That's It
Wait There's More, This Makes You Go On
Waking Up To Find Out What You Want Next
Until One Day You'll Wake Up
Realizing There's Nothing Left Inside And
Nothing Left To Take

Self Satisfied

If I Can See Satisfaction, Could Be Satisfaction
At Its Most Pleasurable Of Moments, Constantly
Would I Then Need To Know Me?
If I Truly Did Know My Self
Would I Always Strive For Satisfaction?
Or Would I Be Content With Myself?
One Must Equate Then Through Trial And Tribulation
To Attain / Obtain Satisfaction And Its Fleeting Moments
From An Equal Time Trying To Find Oneself
That At The End Of The Both Finding Oneself
Would Be The Definition Of Satisfaction

What Is Worth Pain?

Apparently Love
Does Pain Then Give Love Value?
Is This Possible? Can Pain Possibly Be Worth It?
Is Love Supposed To Be Painful?
No, But It Can And Will Be Someday And
When It Eventually Leaves
You'll Find The Only Cure Left When The Pain Arrived
Except If The Love Is For Self
Then The Only Way Your Love
Can Die Is When You Do
Even This Is Questionable

My Values

Values To Think, Behave/Act Upon?
What Is The Most Valuable To You?
How Do You Shape The Above To Get It
Therefore Are Your Behaviors You?
Or Your Desire For A Possession?
For When You Own Something
It Has Already Owned You
It Gave You Brief Happiness And
Comfort When You Got Home
Then You Bragged About It To Your Friends
Then Sat Down Alone And Thought
Of The Amount Of Time You Wasted On A Rock
When Instead You Should've Spent It On Yourself
Funny, You Gave It More Worth Than Self
Tragic, They Give No Worth To Self
Fool, You Thought It The Final Thing, The Perfect Toy
Until One Is Better
Then You Want It Once More
An Endless Cycle Back And Forth
Where Control Is Not Really Yours But
Merely The Cycles' Objects Themselves
That You Spin Around So Fast
To Distract You From The Real Control
That They Have And The Self Control You Already Lost

Where Did You Go?

Where Did You Go?
Where Have You Been Taken?
To Die Today Would Mean A Loss
To See Tomorrow Would Be A Blessing
As Were All Yesterdays
What Could Bring Understanding This To The Forefront?
One With Less Begging For My Opportunity?
One With More To Aspire Toward?
One With Myself Thought And Action Combined
For If I Know Self Betterment I Will Surely Oblige
These Thoughts May Soon Fade Like So Many Times Before
Destructive Action Will Close My Unread Book
Of Words So Important Yet I Refuse To Look
Boasting Confidence And Righteous Self Proclaimed Love
That All Disappears Amongst The Confusion
So I Seek An Old Path, Senseless Delusion
For Little Habits Are Just That
If Delusion's My Habit Then That's What I Am
For It Is The Habits That Form The Man
Of Those Negative Habits I Have Complete Control
Still I Let Them Create The Illusion Of My Soul
My Body Still Seen By The Naked Eye
My Body Lives On But My Soul Wonders Why

Need For Need?

Need Is A Burden On Society
Need Is The Burden Of Society
Impact On An Individual
Impact Of An Individual
Impact Is The Individual
Whatever We Don't Have We Want
Whatever We Have We Don't Want Anymore
All The While We Don't Know What We Want
From Ourselves-- Inside; Feelings Satisfaction
We Want To Improve Our Efficiency At Obtaining An Item
Upon Doing So, We Self –Congratulate
Almost Hinting At Self-Pride
At The Same Time Knowing The Hole Gets Deeper?
The Deeper The Emotion The Deeper The Distraction
The Better The Thought, The Easier The Action
I'll Not Be Defeated
For This Is What I Live For In Turn Stand For
Even If Defeated Pride Still Remains
To Win Once More And Start It Again
What Happened To Those Questions Of Why?
Vanished! Upon Eying The Next Pursuit
True Motivation? Trained Motivation? Self-Motivation?
Actions Indicate All These But
Neglect The Power Of Need
For An Outside Source To Somehow
Inspire/Influence Daily Actions
Time And Time Again You Watch
As This Path Strands You And
Those Around You And Yet You And
They Refuse To Try A New Path
That Although Is Tougher To Travel
Presents A Greater Reward Than Hardship And
If The Reward Is Anything Above Suffering
All Action To Acquire Will Have Proved Their Worth
For Is It Not Proving Our Worth
That Is The Foundation Of Need?

Self Unsolved

Self Involved As Your Self Evolves
My Soul Blends With Life And Slowly Dissolves
A New Problem Rises With Each Problem Solved
Around My Chosen Objects My Mind Revolves
The Revolution Self Buried Still Breathes On
If We Wanted We'd See It But We Think It Has Gone
The Shame Lies In The Superficial Normalcy Created
Looking For Answers That Can't Even Be Calculated
The Game We Play Far Overrated
The Rules From The Start Outdated
Don't You Wonder? Seriously! At Least Once In A While
Is This It?
Would You Say This Is The Creation Of A God?
A Fair One?
One For Justice, Peace, Goodwill, Love?
Or Injustice, War, Evil, Hate?
What Truly Has Been Created
Although Somewhat Sad In This Context Is A Choice
Ultimately We Choose, The Choice Is Our Steps Toward Him
Or Further Away And Likewise From Ourselves
Along With The Purpose Of Our Self

War, Reason

Self-Pride is the friend of war,
Aftermath its outcome.
All Amongst each other
Each against ourselves.
For all those who walk with us,
Against all those who walk beside us.
Blinded by our love to hate
Led by our desire against our fear
Killing to stay alive
If we are truly are alive when we love,
How is killing the same?
By fearing and trying to prevent our own death,
Ending life just the same.
Exploring the capabilities of our souls.
Only finding that our soul is capable
Of the very abandonment from our life
As the life we forced to abandon a soul.

What Is Sought

Unseen Motivation Whether Just Or Not, God May Be Sought
Whether He Appears And I'm There To Greet Is The Question
Heed His Advice Follow His Path,
Become Whole, Become Him, Through Self
So Much I'm Hidden By My Own Hand
It Is With These Hands I Must Find Inner Courage
To Stop Continual Division And Contradiction Of Nature
For If Divisible,
One
Cannot Be Itself But Becomes Merely The Reflection Divided
Infinitely In Reluctant Destiny
In That God Disappears
Then One Questions Justice
Rather Than What Is Sought

Here We

So Here We Are
What Have We Become?
What Have We Made Of Ourselves
Of The Greatest Gift; What Have We Made
Instead Of Achievable Greatness
Opting For The Sweetness Of Destruction
For If Not Sweet Why Proceed?
Let Not The Actions Of Men Be The Action Of Man
So Is This March Yet The Footsteps
A Guided Path Darker With Each Print
Until One Day Our Love For Destruction
Will Stare Us Down With Permanent Gaze
Then We Will Be Forced To Ask How
Yet Through It All We Knew
The Fear Who's Hand We Clench On This March
The Means That Should Precipitate Our Rise Against
Casually Holds Us Against Our Will
Or So The Excuse, The Quantification, Rather Justification
For All Of This And Yet Almost Determined
For However Unjust The Only Shallow Security We Know
This Mechanism Become Machine To Show It's Output
In One Moment The One We Have Blinded Ourselves From
Surely The Only One We Will See
The True Product Alas
The Knowledge It Was Wrong All Along,
We Were Wrong All Along
Let Right Walk To The Forefront
Sadly It's Too Late To Become One With All That Is Wrong With
Mankind,
Man Itself
Fear The Only Excuse
Only If No Other Option Ever Existed

Still Confused?

Everyone Wonders What To Do With Their Life
Not Everyone Is Confused
The Question Is Did You Want Something You Can Never Have?
Yes Perfection!
Why Must We Seek The Abundance Not Yet Found?
Although Anything Can Be Found
If The Search Is In The Right Place
Have You Looked Inside?
That Is Where Your Hiding
That Is Where To Find You
Nothing You'll Find Will Be Abundant And You Will Realize
Your Self Is More Valuable Than Perfection Itself!
Your Self Is Perfection!
My Endless Stomach

Touch Death, It Is Close Enough,
It Is Touching You With The Hand Of Life

Objects Taking Precedence Over Self-Improvement
The Comforting Blanket Also Blocks The State Of Comfort

Blame Itself Is A Weakness
Weakness Is Not An Excuse It's a Choice

Judge Not Your Reflections But Your Projections
Do They Show The Pain In Your Mind?

Be Careful What You Want For This Is Your Heart
 The Final Defense, A Karmic Jury Ponders Your Verdict

Social Opinion

Is Society Its People Or Its Opinion?
Or The Opinion Of A Chosen Few?
You Were Almost Certain It Was The Opinion Of You
This Scope Is Beyond My Friend
Tens Of Billions Of People
Think About That, Thousands Of Which Are Your Relatives
Hundreds Of Which Your Blood And The Others The Same
How Did This Happen?
We Let It Happen, We Wanted It To Happen
Society That Is
Who Do We Impress?
Better Yet What Do We Show?
The Ability To Selectively Love And Selectively Destroy
What Is Better Or Worse For Us?
To Die For Another But Kill The Rest
This May Seem Like Control
If We Controlled These Tendencies Wouldn't Love Be Natural?
Could Evil Not Be Natural Also?
Depends On You, Depends On Society, Depends On Choice
Yes The Choice To Love Evil, Blindly Mind You
Because Everyone Else Does; Let The Conscience Of Others
Be The Decision Of Yours
There's That Control Again
So I Wonder Then, Who's Doing The Thinking? Nobody?
So If We're Not Thinking And All Is Normal And Normal Is Evil
Evil Will Think For Us Until It Dies With You
Unless You Pass It On
Is Society Its People?
Yes Society Is Evil
Whether They Agree Or Not
Their Actions Speak Their Opinion.

There Is Always Risk In Dreams For
That Is What Makes Them Dreams
Risk Is What Will Bring You Closest To Reality On Your Way
For In Conquering You Will Find Out Who You Are
In Doing So Live The Reality
Once Before Only Dreamed Of

The Comfort Of Lies Will Not Replace Guilt
The Discomfort Of Guilt Must Not Invoke Lies

There Is Strength In Adversity,
There Is Adversity In Weakness

If People Must Die For Me To Maintain My Existence;
Then I Myself Am Death And As Is Death,
To Myself I Am Feared And Unknown

We Have As Much Reason To Love Death As We Do To Fear It

Desire And Satisfaction Will Always Stay Ahead Of You
Truly What You Desire Will Never Satisfy
Unless Love Is Your Desire

Your Soul Needs No Possession Besides Itself

Pleasures' Plunder Will Not Sustain,
Soon Destruction Will Create The Same Addiction
In A Desperate Grab At The Feeling
Already Destroyed. Strangely Enough;
By Humanity's Shallow Definition
It Never Existed. Just Like Us

Going Too Far We Pass The Escape We Crave,
Simultaneously The Trap Closes On Us,
The Lies From So Many Times Before Shine
Through As The Light Fades

The Older I Get The More I Figure Out,
I'll Never Be Old Enough To Stop Figuring Things Out
I Have Figured Out I'm Not Old Enough Yet

What Is The Confirmation Of Love?
Someone To Love You More Than Themselves?
That Proof Being Their Death For You?
Upon This Moment The Confirmation That Love Is Only Suffering
Of A Magnitude Which Cannot Be Equated During Its Blindness
Open Eyes To Those Who Do Not Believe
Nor Seek Confirmation Except From Within Themselves

The Old And Grey Man Before You Is You;
A Mirror Less Reflection Of An Extinguished Soul
The Mindless Fire Rages.
Its Weak Attempt At Eternity Fueled By An Everlasting
Hollowness
Emptiness The Cure, An Internal Mirror, Its Reflection Has No Use
For When The Soul Is Seen Eyes Are No Longer Adequate Nor Qualified

Occupation- Defined As What Occupies A Persons Time.
A Person Defined By What Occupies Them.
Truly Defined By What The Time Lost Gets Them

This World Will Swallow Us If It Means Self-Destruction
At Least Our Mouths Will Be Stuffed By What We Ate So Long.
We Will Spread The Disease So Far, Beyond Our Scope, Beyond Reason,
Confusion Reigns Over Imminent Suicide

If Ego's Pleasure Is So Good Why Does It Always Disappear?
So It Is Always In Demand The Only Time It's Not Is When It
Appears

What Keeps Me Here?
Inside This Reality Inside This Cage
My Boundless Soul Somehow Contained
By A Wall I Myself I Choose To Surround
By A Wall Myself I Know I Can Tear Down
Revealing A Truth, The Truth On The Other Side
That Truth Itself Is To Be Without, To Look Deep Inside
If I Look Deep Inside What Will I See?
I Will See Nothing, I Will See Me!

Do Not Let In God, Let Him Be Revealed, Do Not Expect God,
Discover Him, He Is Inside You, You Are The Saviour You Are
Salvation

Pain Gives Fear Great Pleasure, A Justification Of Presence Reaffirmed

Careful This March, Careful In Every Step
To Take Care, Notice, Recognize Importance
Become The Step Each Step Creating A Path
Knowing Each Step Has Value To All Others
Especially To The Ones Not Yet Taken

Unfortunately Fundamental Truths Do Not Arrive By Conventional Mean

The Unknown Is A Basis And Catalyst For Fear
Yet The Further Into My Unknown Self I Travel,
A Catalyst For The Destruction Of Fear Develops
An Almost All-Consuming Desire For This Fears End
Gives Desire A Property That Until Now,
Cast The Dark Shadows That Made Seeing Myself Impossible

Soldiers Of Love

Look At Us, Look At What We've Done
Look What We've Accomplished Separate, But One
March Through This Life Blind But With Some Purpose
Is Our Purpose Beyond Ourselves?
Or Is It Materials And Outer Worship?
Don't Those Who March Have A Greater Cause?
Through All This Marching Have We Once Paused?
To Know We Are Great And There Is A World The Same.
To Be Soldiers We Must Live Up To The Name
We've Grown Into This Role But Is It Just Physically?
For The Strongest Man Is Not If He Is Not Mentally
So With This The Question Is Asked
As A Soldier Are You This Task?
Take On The World For You Are Marching Anyway
Take On Your World Every Single Day
For When Your World Is In Order You Begin To Work On Ours
This Is The First Recognition Of Power
Do Not March Against The World
For You May Get Lost In What To Do
March With The Strength Of A World
Then A World Will March With You

Married To Pain

We Don't Want Pain Yet It Is Our Life
Unwanted Marriage Yet A Perfect Wife
How Can I Detach And Move On?
To The Wife I Wanted All Along
These Glimpses Of Pleasure Only End The Same
I End Up Back In What I Became But
It Is Not What I'll Become
Because Something Calls, That As Of Now I'm Unsure
That Uses Light To Kill Darkness And Make Me Pure
However Elusive It Can Be Found
Despite The Chains By Which I'm Bound
This Calling Inside Is Getting To Loud
My Falling Inside Makes Me Proud
One Day This Pride Will Be Who I Become
The Day My Lie Will Become None
In This Nothingness I Can Rejoice
Because What Was Once Just Loud Is Now My Voice

Pure Provocation

A Provocation Of Purity
The Pinnacle Of Maturity
How Can I Get There With No Before?
A Thoughtless Dispute Is Now A War
How Did I Get Here?
Moreover How Will I Get Back?
In My Darkened Mind I Can Only React
Praying For Light To Shine On Me
Instead Of Letting What Is In Me Be
In This Rebirth I Can Sit With Love
Instead Of Waiting For Something Above
For It Will Never Come When I Expect And Wait
Because In This I Am Only My Fate
I Can Welcome Death Or Find The Light
Both Are Born But One Without Might
The One That Is Pure And Is Not Rehearsed
This One The Cure,
This Is My Birth

Fundamentals

When Your Fundamental Truth Is A Lie
Underlying Truth Is Beyond The Eye
Still You Don't Know What's Behind The Eye
Because The Mind Caused It To Die
Now You Wander A Beaten Path
That Almost All Walk, As You Have So Long
A Mindless Dancer To Societies Song
But Wait! A Note To A Classic Hymn
For Yourself That's Not Complete But Draws You In
To One Day Hear The Masters Call
The One Residing Within Us All
Although You Stumble You Never Fall
Just Lose Sight Of The Path Yet Always Come Back
Abandoning The Beaten Track
For One That's Fresh And Yet So True
To The One That Leads You Back To You

A Man I Know

There Is A Man I Know But Have Not Met
A Man I Will Be But Am Not Yet
I Know My Destiny Is To Meet One Day
Now It Seems I've Found The Way
I Searched High And This Got Me Far
Yet Realized Going Lower And Deeper
You Find Out Who You Really Are
There Was A Lot There I Didn't Want To Know
Without This Knowledge I Could Not Grow
It Had A Power To Make Me Blind
As Pain Can Be Tough To Face
Only When I Got There Could I See This Place
Although Dark And Cold, It Was Still Me
As I Realized Blind And Cold
Was Not What I Wanted To Be
So I Lit A Candle That Started A Fire,
Made Loving Light My Only Desire
As Much Effort I Used To Make Myself Lost
Is What I Will Use To Find Myself At All Cost
For This Journey No Price Is To High
There Is No Other To Finish Before I Die
Wasting Time I Cannot Afford
For Every Moment Can Take Me Closer
To The Greatest Reward
The Reward Of Me, Of Being, Of Love
To Know I Earned The One Thing That Is Real
Although Not The Flame Yet, The Fire I Can Feel
Still A Flame Nonetheless,
Witnessing The Darkness Burn By My Hand
Getting To Know Something That All Should Understand
That Darkness Can Win But Only If You Let It
Light It On Fire For The Reward, Go Now And Get It
Meet The Greatest Man Who Ever Lived
To Do This All Of You Is What You Must Give
Then You Can Meet This Great Man And See His Face
When The Old You Leaves With The Darkness
Then This Great Man Will Take His Place

Soul Eyes

I've Looked Hard At My Soul And
At The Things By Which I Am Obsessed
To Know I Know Not My Soul, My Self,
Nor The Objects I Possess
A Conclusion Has Been Drawn But One That Leaves Room
That Although Progressing, My Life Is Consumed
Not By A Constant Gaze Into My Self But
The Perpetual Creation Of Something Else
A Body Who's Footsteps Take Much Time
In Pursuit Of All But The Foundation Of Mind
Rather In Pursuit Of What Of My Mind I Have Found
Aside From It Being There I Know Little More
Can This Be Considered Foundation?
Could It Be I Become What I Am Not
Rather Than Who I Am?
Worse Yet Being The Constant Catalyst For This
In Each Moment Directed Towards, And Yet I March
Direction Unknown,
I Do Know I Detest Pain Yet I Require It
For If Not Why It's Timely Appearances.
My Requirement For Pleasure Merely A Reflection Of This
Sometimes Its Exact Double, ME
Will I Find The State At Which I Thirst No More
May My Exact Double Become Pleasured
By The Decrease In Pleasure Itself?
Then Again How Would I Know This Path?
It Is Yet To Be Walked
It Lays Itself Before Me In Gold At All Times
Whereas Now The Gold I Seek,
Upon Looking Back Turns To Clay But
The Gold Remains In Front Evermore.
This Unwalked Path However I Somehow Know
That Upon Looking Back
At Footsteps Taken Will Remain Golden
Furthermore I Will Become It
As It Leads Me To Nothingness, To Where I Came From,
Where I Should Have Never Left And Where I Should Be

Who Am I To Judge God?

For When I Stare At Death And Disease I Wonder Why?
Where Is The Beauty In This?
What Great Creator Would Create Such?
What Of This Love I Am To Be,
Resides In Famine And War?
In This Darkness Only Lies A Gateway To Disbelief

Then I Am Told God Is In Us All

Strange As It Seems, Few Welcome This Pestilence
I Guess Enough Nonetheless
Enough To Make It Exist
I Wonder Without Me Would The Universe Exist?
Would I Without It?

Then I'm Told God Is In Us All

Strange Now A Penetration
For Amongst This There Is Peace,
There Is Beauty, Everywhere
Could Evil Be Beautiful?
Is It Not A Product Of God?
For If We Are A Part Of God And
We Allow It To Exist Does Not God Also?
In God's Make Up Is God Not Perfect/Beautiful?

Then I Think God Is In Us All

Now Surely There Is A Plan
That Almost All Do Not Know But
Mostly Know It Must Exist
Does This Plan Allow For Beauty And Evil To Coexist?
Or Does It Lie In The Perception Thereof?

For To The Evil Man Is Not Beauty Evil?
To The Man Of Beauty Is Not
Evil, Evil And Beauty, Beauty?
So Then Is It Reasoning/Perception?
Or Is It Lack Of The Blueprint?

One Thing We Do Know Is We Are In The Blueprint

Then I Feel God Is In Us All

For Me To Put A Higher Trust In Myself
Than The Man Of Evil
Would Be An Injustice For In This I Am Judging
In This Judging My Belief Can Be Lost
So Now If I Am To Judge Much Less
Feel Worthy To Judge God
Then Surely I Must Be Higher Than
Or At Least Think I'm Better Than But
Then I Ask Does God Ask These Questions Of Himself?
Or Has He Based Future On
Putting Judgment On Its Shelf?
Or Disowned Judgment Of The Self?
In This Now Is Perfect Health
For Me To Know God I Must Not Judge
For In Judging God I Only Judge Myself

Now I Know God Is In Us All
Now I Know God Is In All
Now I Know God Is All
Now I Know All Is In Me
Now I Know What God Meant Us To See
To See All Without Judgment
God Is What We Will Be

The Sweetest Fruit

Strangely It Seems That In My Waking Life
That Although My Eyes Are Open,
Much Of What I See Is Fruitless And Limited
When Sleeping My Eyes Are Closed,
What I See Is Limitless And Although It Bears Fruit
I Am Not Of the Capacity To Taste
In Both Of These Lives I Long For Something More
Now Realizing Something More Exists
However Limited My Vision, I Know It Is Something
I Can Taste Without Even Touching
My Arms Welcome It, But As Of Now
Feel Not It's Embrace, My Eyes Welcome It,
Yet They Look Into Empty Space
How Am I To Find What Cannot Be Seen?
I Must Change How I Look And What I Look With
At This Moment I Will Taste Fruit Smaller
Yet More Bountiful Than All Others Tasted Combined
It's Seed Harvested Within Myself
Through Only Belief That I Can Grow
Whereas Before Non-Belief Prevented
Now Slowly A Leaf Fights To Find The Light
That Is Rightfully It's Own.

Many Obstacles Appear, As They Did Before
Although Many, Overcoming Them Becomes Easier
With The Knowledge, That I Will One Day Have A
Trunk And Many Branches With Many Leaves
Reaching For All Light, Now My Obstacles Less
Seeming So Long Ago I Was Merely A Seed
As The Light Seems Endless And My Leaves Plenty
There Is No Comparison To The Roots That Have
Penetrated The Depths Of My Soul
Although These Depths May Be Endless
That I May Not See The Light I
Truly Wanted To Before I Die,
I'll Know That With Eyes Closed
I Will Have Seen The Brightest Light Possible And
Will Have Become The Fruit I Before
Only Blindly Reached For.

Serving A Man, Serving Mankind, Serving Soul, Serving State, Serving Is....

All One In The Same
All Is One, This One Has No Name
Yet We Give It One, I Hope Only To Describe
For No Words Are Worthy Of Scribe
Action Remains The Only Value
Tell Me Do You Take The Words And
Thoughts Of Man As Truth?
Or As It Does… Might You Crave A Solid Truth
Thus This Word-Scarred State Does As Well
If Words Are To Be Used, They Are
As The Feeble Communication, But Still A
Form Needed In Order To Guide.
Makes Me Wonder, Without Speech Where We Might Be,
This Again Is Of No Consequence, But Where We Are
In This Moment Is. Still The Return To Action,
All Is Perfect And Truth Should Not Be Judged And
Is Not, Merely The Thought Of Evil Is
Actioned For Or Against, As Is Good
Therefore Judging Is Not Judging…. Is Action
Is This The Non-Judgment Spoken Of Throughout Time
As The Attainment/Ability Necessary To
Be …Is… The State… What We Call God?
God/Us Does/Should Not Have What We May Call "Time"
To Judge For It Only Acts Just Like Us… As Us
As We Are In All Ways A Part Of God But
Will We Recognize How To Be (Act) As/Like God?
Judging, The Terminology Used, This Word Only
Describes The Merger Of Moment And Action Therefore
It Cannot Be Revisited For The Value In Doing So Passes
Exactly In That Moment So The Use Of Time
Lacks Merit Also. What Delusion!
So This Known It's Shell Can Be Cracked And Importance
Focused On Becoming The State And Nothing Else.
Placing Relevance On The State And What We Describe As
A Moment. Therein Lies The Challenge… Each Moment.
As All Is The State. Then Giving The Self (As Described By Us)
To The State Which Also Includes Giving The Self Properly

Back To Its' Self For Dissection, By Moments, In Order To
Return To The State. This Being So, Any Activity Towards
What May Be Deemed Lesser, Equal, Or More Is Nothing But
An Activity To The State Itself. Therein, As Well, Lies
The Choice From Within To Improve The Positivity Of
The Levels Of What The State Has Created,....
It As A Whole. So Technically Could Not The
Action Of "Serving" Perceived Justice Not Be A
Grave Injustice? This Question Answered, Points To This
Serving Of The State Through What Is Called "You,"
Which Is The State Itself In So Doing You Become
You And In This Where Do You Find Room To Judge?
It Is Impossible! Becoming The State Is The Self Disappeared.
Only After The Self Sees Itself, Rather Acts Itself
As The State. Thus Natural As This Is What The State Is…
True Nature
Selfless
Not Itself,
Merely It,
You

Even Death Is Something. Surely Life Is

What Can One Man Do?
A Question Many Have Asked
Is Your Reply Nothing?
In This View You Can Do Something, That Being Die
Why Not?
In Nothing There Is No Purpose
Even In Death There Is Purpose And Yet Not
In Your Life?
Then Die… Go On Die
In Fact Kill… Kill This Thought Of You And Your
Ability Being Nothing
Your Coffin Somehow Sealed?
Yet Not Even Closed?
You Must See Some Power?
You've Given Nothing A Chance For So Long And
Look At You Now, You Still Think You Are Nothing
Ever Wonder The Possibility Of Thinking
You Are Something?
Do It Now, And Again, And Again
Continue This. Look Now At What You've Become
Not That Crazy Of A Concept Is It?
If Your Answer Is Yes,
You've Already Abandoned Nothing,
You've Already Stepped Toward Something
Get What Something Is?   You!
Although Only One, Something Is Still Something
Now What If A Group Of Somethings Got Together?
They Would Remain One
As One Not Zero Or Nothing But
One, Something. Could You Imagine The Power
They Could Witness?
Maybe The Power To Kill Nothing Once And For All
To Kill Themselves And Any Others
Who Like They Used To, Think They Are Nothing.
What A Glorious Suicide
What A Glorious Death
In This Death A Purpose…
Life Itself.

Humanity's Fondness For Difference Is Perplexing, Love Is Not

If A Man Is To Set About A Task, A Life, There Is Potential For
Gratification Upon Completion In The Knowledge That He Has
Done So By His Own Accord. Is The Humble Man He Who Thanks
Those Besides Who Make/Made It Possible?
From Father/Mother And So On?
Or Rather Is He One Who Holds Near A Simple Concept That He
Among All Of Man Knows That Without All Man He Would Be But
One Man, As He Is Now, Except Again,
In This State One Amongst Many Men.

Conversely Without Him Mankind,
In It's Form, Would Be Different.
Can Any More Or Less Importance Be Placed Upon Him Or Even
The Sum Of Men? Without The Others Would Less Need Be
Placed By Him, For Him, On The Accomplishment For Him In
Perceived Positive Creation From Outer And Inner Destruction? His
Perceived Gratification Possibly Being A Negative Effect On Others
Yet Somehow Still Accepted As A Move Toward Positivity By Him.
Yet Most Of The Time Not By Others. Strangely Enough Mostly
What He Tries To Display May Make The Others Wish He Was Not
Able To Display It And Further That They Could Themselves In An
Ongoing Pattern And Cycle Of Jealousy, Pride, Hate....Ego

This Is The Heart Of Separateness That In Lust Breeds. Oddly
Enough Through This Lust He Fools Himself Into Thinking He Is
Bettering For Mankind And Creating A Commonality For Them
When In Reality He Is Creating A Common Goal With Only His
Ego. We Must Realize Egos' Capability To Destroy When The
Opposite Should Be True. Yet We Let It Have Residence Within Us.
Should Mankind Expect Anything Besides Destruction Of Itself
If It Chooses This? It Seems As If Most Favor This Activity. Even If
This Is The Only Activity It Is Still Not Truth
For Truths' Common Is Only Love.

Shouldn't A Man's Direction Toward Accomplishment Be In
Common With All Man?
In So Doing Does Not Separateness,
Destruction And Ego Disappear?

Further In The Constant Appearance Of Separating, Destroying
And Ego, Is He Not Witness To The Tendency Toward Creative
Destruction Of Those Who Themselves Perpetuate Its Creation? The
Answer Must Be Known For Surely If One Was To Witness, Ceasing
Would Be The Only Logical Action. However Impossible Seeming,
Denying This Is Conducted And Condoned.
Truly, Perplexing.

So Now Can It Not Be Said That The Opposite (Commonality,
Oneness) Would Perpetuate/Create Positivity? In This Life We Are
But In Constant Moments That Form The Energy Around Us And
In Us. If One Is To Talk Of A World Of No Control, This We Still
Control In This We Must Know That Through This Control. We
Welcome All Positive Or Negative Energy By Our Hand. Therefore
Can It Be Said That This Formation By Choice Of Energy Is Of
Negativity? If In Denial Of This, An Invitation Is Sent To Those
Who Deny, To View Their Own State To See If Negativity Resides.
If They Are Love, Then Nothing Is Present Except Love. However
All Besides Is Admittance To The Negativity They Choose For
Themselves, Thus Mankind.

So Then Can It Be Said An Action Toward Being In Anything Besides
Love Is An Action Toward Negativity? In This Then Can It Be Said
That Action In This Regard (If Commonality Can Now Be Granted
Worth) Is Action Toward Negativity/Destruction To Mankind? Then
Perhaps Why Love Is Not Chosen Is Simply That Separateness Is.
In This, No Experience Of Love Is Brought Forth. Therefore Again
Denying The Being Of What The Very Foundation Of The Being
Should Be Made Of And As Well Mankind. Most Need Only Their
Own Life And The State Of Mankind To Find The Validity Of This
Argument. Simply Then, The More Of Mankind, That Is Closer
To This, The Closer Mankind Is To Perpetual Negativity. Can We
Now See The Perplexity Of The Denial Of Truth, Love, Being And
Oneness We Ourselves Can Choose For Not Just Ourselves But For
Those We Must Now Deem As Common?

When Perception Shifts Toward Oneness A Greater Need For
Love Now Perpetuates. In Common Is An Equation Beyond
Comprehension By Variables. We Control The Metamorphosis Of
This Equation, Of Self… Mankind
So Now When One Is Of The Knowledge Of The Importance Of

Love And Then Can See In Him This Root Forming Does It/ Can
It Recognize The Seed Still? Surely It Must. Made And Planted
By One Who Before Him Recognized Commonality In Love By
His Action That Now Caused The Other To Find In Himself A
Causation Toward This Now Being His Action. Now The Fading Of
Separateness To Something More Pure; Oneness… Love.

Now Creation Can Be Made Genuine, Worthy And Whole
So Through Himself He Becomes The Proof Of Actions Previous
And Action Future Thus Creating The Common Present Love In
Which Nothing Besides In Him Has Residence.

In This Being His Home And This Home Being Him, Is Not
Commonality Defined? Through This We Can See That Nothing
Has Stronger Definition Than Love.
Surely Now Any Choice Besides Must Also Be
The Definition Of Perplexing.

This Choice Requires One Man Although Others May Contribute
To This Choice In Self Love They Are Not Necessarily Required.
This May Be The One Separation Granted Worth If Ignoring The
Fact That His Choice For Self Love Contributes To Ours As Well. If
You Crave Separateness Then Let It Be For Separation From Those
Who Do Not Love. Remember However You Were Once Them And
Now The Duty Of Commonality Has Been Bestowed Upon You To
Love Those Who May As Of Now Choose Not To Love, Even Hate
Others, Including You.

However In So Doing Do Not Be Surprised If You Find That The
One Who Before Like You Did Not Love Now Stands Before You As
One Who In Common Now Loves, Himself, You And Mankind.

Perfecting The "A"

To As Far As It Goes
One Must Know How Far It Goes.
If It Is To Be Said You Are The "A," It Is True.
If I Say I Am The "A," I Am Also Speaking Truth.
So Is One A Lie?
Or Are Both Truth?
Simply, One Proclaiming A Lie In The Other
Is Himself Living The Lie He Proclaims In The Other
One Who Sees Both As "A" Steps To Truth, In Oneness
In Separation There Is No "A" But Residence In "B"
Placing Yourself Or Another In "B"
Still Implies Existence
However In This Form It Is Illusion. So Explains Most.
Explore.
For If To Be One, There Is No Other.
If All Is One Therein Lies Extreme
Importance In All Moments And
All Aspects Thereof; Thought, Belief, Action.
Refinement Toward Positivity Of Each.
For If Moments Are Unified, As One,
Then Collectively The Sum Is
The Contribution To The "A"
So Then Your Contribution To You
Is Contribution To Me, All
This Is How Far It Goes, Forever
Yes Reflect Now, Imagine The Power Of This, You.
It Then Must Be A Force Toward Positive Graduation
It's Pinnacle Being Love!
So How Then Can One Love Another
Without Loving The "A?" Them?
How Can One Love Themself Without Loving The Other?
Be This Love And We Are Instantly The Love You Give Us.
Likewise Us To You,
But Not In Obligation Or Necessity, Just Mutual
In This Our Beauty Refined
In This Our Duty Defined
In This How Far The "A" Can Go
It Cannot Go As Far If It Stops At You
To Let It Go, Letting In Love Is All We Need To Do.

The Fate Of Loneliness

No My Friend You Are Not Alone
There Are No Walls To Hold You In But
You're Still In A Home
You Can Walk Out The Door
Instead Of Looking Out The Window
Wandering Around The Depths Of Your Mind
Yes Friend Walk Out The Door And Lock It Behind
Then Raise The Walls And Keep
In There What Kept You In
What Before Trapped You There On The Brink Of Ruin
All You Had To Do Was Change Yours' And Its' Place
To Watch The Frown You Once Bore Cover Its' Face
Now Not Alone But One With It All
Now Right At Home With The Rest Of It All
Now The Home Is Inside Of You
Now It's The Mind That Has Nothing To View

Forest

Explore Your Decisions And Outcomes
Could It Be Said That The Thought Behind
The Decision Was The Relative Make-Up Of The Outcome?
For If In The Decision Is A Pre-Conceived Notion
It Is Just That, Prior To Conception
So Then, What Is Just Before Conception
Is The Root Of Conception Itself
If The Next Step Is Conception Are We To Believe
In The Possible Disappearance In The Root And
Somehow A Tree Might Grow Differently Or At All?
Or If The Root Has The Make-Up Of Dark
That The Tree May Grow Light?
Thus In Your Decisions The Near Exactness Of The Outcome
Now Then What Can Be Said Of Those Who Allow
Others To Make Their Decisions?
What If He Who Decides For The Other Is Himself
The One With Infected Roots, Branches And Seeds?
Could Not These Seeds Be Planted In The Other?
Could Not This Tree Grow In Him Too?
If So, Would These Seeds Be Expected To Do
Anything But Grow Into Further Infection?
Yet The Acceptance, And In This How
Quickly A Forest Grows
Every Once In A While Though, Through Different
Shades Of Light, An Example Of Another Tree In The
Forest And Other Forces, A Tree May Choose To Break
From Its Bloodlines And Those Of His Forest.
It Gains The Power To Fight Off This Infection And
Through It's Bravery Its Seeds Become Like It
An Example Of The Light To Take In
To Become The Beginnings Of A New Forest
So In This Your Thought Must Become
To Take In Proper Light
Before Each Decision And In This The Make-Up
Of The Forrest You Will Live In

Printed in the United States
125496LV00001B/42/P

9 780595 528899